THE

Gutsy
Girl's

DEVOTIONAL

JoAnne Simmons

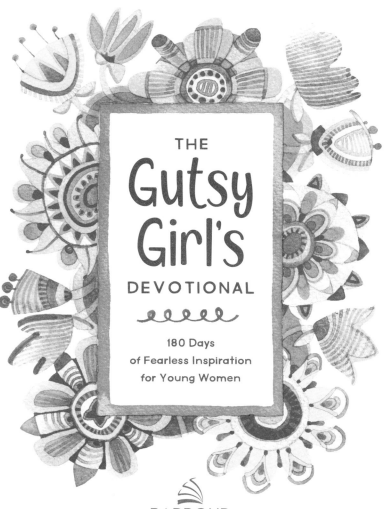

THE
Gutsy
Girl's
DEVOTIONAL

180 Days
of Fearless Inspiration
for Young Women

BARBOUR
PUBLISHING

Member of the
Evangelical Christian
Publishers Association

Printed in China.

Introduction

Celebrate your weakness!

Um. . .what? you might be thinking. *I thought this was a book about being strong and gutsy and living fearlessly.*

Yes, it is! And you read that first line right. God said this to the apostle Paul in the Bible: "My grace is all you need. My power works best in weakness" (2 Corinthians 12:9 NLT).

Paul wrote in response: "So now I am glad to boast about my weaknesses, so that the power of Christ can work through me. That's why I take pleasure in my weaknesses, and in the insults, hardships, persecutions, and troubles that I suffer for Christ. For when I am weak, then I am strong" (2 Corinthians 12:9–10 NLT).

What God taught Paul about being weak is for you to learn today too. No matter how humanly strong you might strive to be, it could never compare to the strength and power of the one true almighty God who created the world and everything in it—including you and all your gifts and abilities.

So read on and let these devotionals help you draw closer to the one who made you and loves you more than anyone else ever could, the one who is the source of all real and lasting strength and courage. He is the only one who can make you a genuinely gutsy girl.

The Story about Paul, Part 1

*Meanwhile, Saul was uttering threats with every breath and was eager
to kill the Lord's followers. . . . As he was approaching Damascus on
this mission, a light from heaven suddenly shone down around him.
He fell to the ground and heard a voice saying to him, "Saul! Saul!
Why are you persecuting me?" "Who are you, lord?" Saul asked. And
the voice replied, "I am Jesus, the one you are persecuting! Now get
up and go into the city, and you will be told what you must do."*
ACTS 9:1, 3–6 NLT

Why does it matter what the apostle Paul said in the Bible? Why should
we listen to and learn from him and the letters he wrote? Well, he's a big
deal with a big story. He started out known as Saul, a man who was very
religious, but he hated and killed those who believed in Jesus. But then in
a dramatic moment on the road to Damascus, Jesus stopped Paul in his
tracks and changed him completely.

**Dear God, help me to learn from Paul's story and example and his
writings. Show me how You can work in dramatic ways in people's
lives. Help me to always be brave enough to let You work in my life
to change anything in me that You see needs to change. Amen.**

The Story about Paul, Part 2

Instantly something like scales fell from Saul's eyes, and he regained his sight. Then he got up and was baptized. . . . Saul stayed with the believers in Damascus for a few days. And immediately he began preaching about Jesus in the synagogues, saying, "He is indeed the Son of God!" All who heard him were amazed. "Isn't this the same man who caused such devastation among Jesus' followers in Jerusalem?" they asked. "And didn't he come here to arrest them and take them in chains to the leading priests?" Saul's preaching became more and more powerful, and the Jews in Damascus couldn't refute his proofs that Jesus was indeed the Messiah.
ACTS 9:18–22 NLT

After God dramatically stopped Paul from his evil deeds, He caused Paul to go blind for a few days. With the help of a man named Ananias, God worked a total transformation in Paul and then restored his sight. Soon Paul was a brand-new person who began spreading the good news that Jesus is the Son of God. He helped many people to believe in Jesus as our one and only Savior, and through his writings in the Bible, he is still helping people become believers even today.

Dear God, when I see others who are strongly opposed to You, give me courage and hope by reminding me of Paul's story. Remind me that nothing is impossible with You, almighty God! Amen.

So. . .Have You? Part 1

"Believe in the Lord Jesus and you will be saved."
ACTS 16:31 NLT

Let's be clear: You can't be a truly gutsy girl, full of God's Spirit and power, unless you have accepted Jesus Christ as your Lord and Savior. So. . .have you? Let these questions and scriptures help you figure it out:

- Do you believe that there is only one true God? (Isaiah 44:6; 46:9)
- Do you believe that Jesus is God and came to earth as a baby to live a perfect human life? (Hebrews 4:15; 1 Peter 2:21–22)
- Do you admit that you make mistakes and are a sinner? (Romans 3:23; 1 John 1:8–10)
- Do you believe Jesus died on the cross to forgive you of your sin? (Romans 5:6–11; 1 Peter 3:18)
- Do you believe Jesus rose to life again and offers eternal life to all who believe in Him as the one and only Savior from sin? (Romans 10:9; 1 Corinthians 6:14; 1 Peter 1:3; 1 John 5:4)
- Do you believe you should give your life to Jesus and live it for Him, following His ways? (Romans 6:1–14)

Even if you're not sure yet, you can keep on thinking and praying about these things. Continue to read God's Word and ask Him to guide you, plus talk to people you know who love Jesus and ask them for help.

Dear God, I want to be saved from my sin! Please help me believe, and then please grow my faith in You. Amen.

So. . .Have You? Part 2

For God so loved the world that he gave his one and only Son,
that whoever believes in him shall not perish but have eternal life.
For God did not send his Son into the world to condemn the world,
but to save the world through him. Whoever believes in him is not
condemned, but whoever does not believe stands condemned already
because they have not believed in the name of God's one and only Son.
JOHN 3:16–18 NIV

If your answer to all those questions in part 1 of this devotional is truly yes and you have prayed to God about your answers to those questions and asked Jesus into your life, then

- you are saved from your sin;
- you have the promise of life forever in heaven; and
- in this world you have the help and power and courage of God's Holy Spirit within you every second of every day!

Dear Jesus, I admit my sin and my need for You. I believe that You are God and that You lived a sinless human life on earth. You died on the cross to cover all of my sin. Then You rose again, and You give me eternal life and constant help and power through Your Holy Spirit. I believe in You as my one and only Savior! I can't ever thank You enough, and I will praise You forever! Amen.

Be Gutsy and Get Baptized

Jesus came and said to them, "All authority in heaven and on earth has been given to me. Go therefore and make disciples of all nations, baptizing them in the name of the Father and of the Son and of the Holy Spirit, teaching them to observe all that I have commanded you. And behold, I am with you always, to the end of the age."
MATTHEW 28:18–20 ESV

If you have accepted Jesus as your Savior, it's important to be baptized. Baptism is a symbol with water that represents getting rid of sin and having new life in Jesus. Baptism shows that you want to obey God and be like Jesus. (Read about His baptism in Matthew 3:13–17; Mark 1:9–11; and Luke 3:21–22.) Baptism shows that you are saved from sin and are a follower of Jesus. Having the courage to get baptized helps inspire others to trust in Jesus as Savior too.

Dear Jesus, I want to have the courage to show others that I love You and believe in You as Savior and want to obey You with my life. Please let my baptism inspire others to accept You as their Savior too. Amen.

By the Power of the Holy Spirit

May the God of hope fill you with all joy and peace in believing,
so that by the power of the Holy Spirit you may abound in hope.
ROMANS 15:13 ESV

If you're ever feeling scared, worried, or anxious (or all of those!) about anything at all but you know you have accepted Jesus as your Savior, then do this: Stop for a moment. Close your eyes. Take a deep breath. Then focus on the fact that the all-powerful, all-knowing Creator God is living in you through the Holy Spirit! Let that truth fill you with peace and confidence. Jesus promised, "If you love Me, you will do what I say. Then I will ask My Father and He will give you another Helper. He will be with you forever. He is the Spirit of Truth. The world cannot receive Him. It does not see Him or know Him. You know Him because He lives with you and will be in you" (John 14:15–17 NLV).

> **Dear God, because I trust in Jesus Christ as my Savior, You are living in me through Your Holy Spirit. Please help me to repeat that fact endlessly in my mind. I don't ever want to forget it. Strengthen me and make me brave again and again with Your great power, courage, love, joy, peace, and hope! Amen.**

Equipped and Empowered by God's Word

All Scripture is God-breathed and is useful for teaching, rebuking, correcting and training in righteousness, so that the servant of God may be thoroughly equipped for every good work.

2 TIMOTHY 3:16–17 NIV

God can communicate any way He wants, and He loves to encourage us in many ways—but especially with words, since He gave us His Word, the Bible. It's His main way of speaking to people. It's not just some ancient book that doesn't matter for today, and it shouldn't just lie around or sit on a shelf collecting dust. It has been changing lives for thousands of years, and it still does today. Hebrews 4:12 8 (NLT) says, "The word of God is alive and powerful." No other book is *living*! That's amazing! So spend time reading God's Word and letting it speak to you. With the combination of the Holy Spirit living and working in you and God's Word in your mind and heart, you are equipped and empowered to face absolutely any problem or hardship or enemy.

Dear God, thank You for communicating, empowering, and equipping through Your Word. Help me to read it, memorize it, use it, and love it. Amen.

Is God's Word Trustworthy?

When you received the word of God, which you heard from us,
you accepted it not as a human word, but as it actually is,
the word of God, which is indeed at work in you who believe.
1 THESSALONIANS 2:13 NIV

You might wonder sometimes, *How do I know the Bible is true? Why should I trust it to equip and empower me?* If you take time to look, you will find amazing research from experts throughout history who verify why the Bible can be trusted far more than any other book ever written. More importantly, constantly remember that you have a relationship with God Himself through Jesus Christ, and you have the Holy Spirit in you. As you read the whole Bible *patiently and consistently over time*, ask God to show more and more of Himself to you through His Word. Ask Him to grow your faith, and then trust Him to do it—and you will be amazed at how He answers your prayers.

Dear God, please keep growing my faith in You as I read Your powerful Word! Show me clearly how and why it's true. Draw me closer to You and help me to love learning from You. Amen.

The Power of Prayer

Don't worry about anything; instead, pray about everything. Tell God
what you need, and thank him for all he has done. Then you will
experience God's peace, which exceeds anything we can understand.
His peace will guard your hearts and minds as you live in Christ Jesus.
PHILIPPIANS 4:6–7 NLT

Prayer is super powerful. It will make you brave and gutsy because you'll draw closer to the one true almighty God when you pray. As you ask Him to give you strength and wisdom and to meet your needs and bless you, don't forget to focus on everything you already have. When you think of the countless ways God has already blessed you and provided for you, you'll realize there is nothing to worry or feel weak about. Just like He has in the past, God will continue to bless you and provide for you—always. Thank Him and praise Him for who He is and all He has done. Then let His amazing peace fill you up and chase away whatever worries and weaknesses you might have.

> Dear God, please remind me how You want to empower me
> through prayer as I draw closer to You! Thank You for all the
> ways You have blessed and helped me and for all the ways
> You will continue to. I praise You! And I trust You in every
> moment for everything I need, today and every day. Amen.

Perfect, Powerful Prayer

He took Peter and the two sons of Zebedee with Him. He began to have much sorrow and a heavy heart. Then He said to them, "My soul is very sad. My soul is so full of sorrow I am ready to die. You stay here and watch with Me." He went on a little farther and got down with His face on the ground. He prayed, "My Father, if it can be done, take away what is before Me. Even so, not what I want but what You want."

MATTHEW 26:37–39 NLV

Jesus gave us the perfect example of powerful prayer, both when He taught us to pray (see Matthew 6:9–13) and when He prayed before He went to the cross. He knew what an awful thing was about to happen to Him, and He was honest that He didn't want to go through with it. But still He prayed, "Not what I want but what You want." He knew His Father's way was best, even if it would be horribly hard at first.

Dear Jesus, thank You for going through such an awful death to save me from my sin. I'm so very sorry and also so very grateful. I'm beyond happy that You rose to life again and gave me eternal life as well! And I'm so grateful for Your examples of prayer. Help me to pray not for what I want but for what our perfect heavenly Father wants, like You did. Amen.

We Need God's Listening Ear

Listen, all you who fear God, and I will tell you what he did for me. For I cried out to him for help, praising him as I spoke. If I had not confessed the sin in my heart, the Lord would not have listened. But God did listen! He paid attention to my prayer.
PSALM 66:16–19 NLT

God knows and hears everything we think and say. But to have total confidence that God not only hears but *listens to* and answers our prayers, we must regularly admit to God when we mess up and disobey and dishonor Him. We have to confess our sins to Him. The Bible is clear that God forgives us and removes our sin as far as the east is from the west (Psalm 103:12), but we need to admit our wrongdoing. That keeps us humble and depending on God, which is the best kind of gutsiness because no one is greater or more powerful than our good and loving Father God!

Dear God, I do make many mistakes, and I don't want to hide them or pretend I'm perfect. These are my sins, Lord:_____.
I confess them to You. Please forgive me and remove my sins from me. Thank You so much that You do! Amen.

Be Gutsy about the Greatest Commandments

"Of all the commandments, which is the most important?"
Jesus replied, "The most important commandment is this: 'Listen,
O Israel! The LORD our God is the one and only LORD. And you must
love the LORD your God with all your heart, all your soul, all your mind,
and all your strength.' The second is equally important: 'Love your
neighbor as yourself.' No other commandment is greater than these."
MARK 12:28–31 NLT

The most important things you need to be gutsy about are the two commandments that Jesus said are the greatest. First, love God with everything that is in you—all your heart, soul, mind, and strength. And second, love your neighbor, meaning anyone around you, the same as you love yourself.

You've probably heard some people say, "Jesus just says to love everyone. That's all that matters about following Him." But they often ignore the fact that He said that before we love others, we are to love God first and most of all. We can't love others in the best ways that God intended unless we first love God with all our heart, soul, mind, and strength—and that includes getting to know Him through His whole Word in context and through prayer.

Dear Jesus, I want to follow Your greatest commandments
to love You first and then love others. Keep teaching me
how, according to Your Word and Your will. Amen.

Be a Bold Young Leader

Command and teach these things. Don't let anyone look down on you because you are young, but set an example for the believers in speech, in conduct, in love, in faith and in purity.

1 TIMOTHY 4:11–12 NIV

Even when you're young, you can be a strong and gutsy leader. You can choose to set an example and show others how to live the best kind of life. You can learn God's Word and follow it. You can choose to love God and others well and show respect and kindness. You can be bold and yet also have humility. You can share the good news of Jesus every chance you get. You can ask for God's wisdom and use it. You can work hard at everything you do as a way to bring praise to God, not yourself. You won't do all this perfectly, and that's okay. But you can try your very best and know that as a young person living your life devoted to God, you are setting a vital and vibrant example for others to follow!

Dear God, even while I'm young, and then every day of my life, please help me to be a strong and gutsy leader because I follow You first and foremost. Amen.

Don't Be Sassy

*Don't use foul or abusive language. Let everything you
say be good and helpful, so that your words will be
an encouragement to those who hear them.*
EPHESIANS 4:29 NLT

Gutsy and *sassy* are descriptions that sometimes go hand in hand. But being sassy with what we say should never be our goal or something to be proud of. Our words matter, and we don't want to be careless or too bold with them. It's super hard to *always* say what is good and helpful. James 3:2 (NLV) says, "We all make many mistakes. If anyone does not make a mistake with his tongue by saying the wrong things, he is a perfect man." In other words, it takes a totally perfect person to *never* make a mistake with words. And there is no perfect person other than Jesus. That's why we need so much help from God through the Holy Spirit to watch what we say. And when we mess up—and we will—we must ask for forgiveness from God and from the ones our words have affected. Thankfully, God loves to forgive and help us, and so we should always want to forgive and help others too.

Dear God, please help me to carefully watch my words. I want to be gutsy and bold for You but in wise and good and helpful ways. Forgive me when I mess this up. Thank You for Your love and grace. Amen.

Noah Was Gutsy

*Noah was a righteous man, blameless among the people
of his time, and he walked faithfully with God. . . .
Noah did everything just as God commanded him.*
GENESIS 6:9, 22 NIV

You probably know the story of Noah and the ark. (You can read all about it in Genesis 6–10.) Imagine for a minute how gutsy it was of Noah to follow God's plans that must have seemed totally crazy! Build a giant ark? Collect two of each animal and load them up along with the family? Then wait while the rains fall and totally flood and destroy the earth? Do you think people walked past his construction site and laughed hysterically at him? Did they spread mean jokes and gossip about him? Even if they did, in the end, what happened? Only Noah and his family were saved from the flood because they listened to God.

Even if God asks you to do things that might seem crazy to others, even if friends laugh at you and gossip about you for following Jesus, obey Him anyway. In the end, you will see how God was working in your life in the best ways.

> **Dear God, help me to be gutsy and obey You, even if it
> seems crazy at first. I trust that You will help me see the
> good plans and happy endings You have for me. Amen.**

He Knows How Weak We Are

We have a great Religious Leader Who has made the way for man to go to God. He is Jesus, the Son of God, Who has gone to heaven to be with God. Let us keep our trust in Jesus Christ. Our Religious Leader understands how weak we are. Christ was tempted in every way we are tempted, but He did not sin. Let us go with complete trust to the throne of God. We will receive His loving-kindness and have His loving-favor to help us whenever we need it.

HEBREWS 4:14–16 NLV

There's no use pretending we have it all together and are doing everything right in life. Jesus knows the truth. When we admit and embrace our weaknesses and depend fully on our Savior who knows exactly what it's like to live a human life, that's when we have all that we need to power through our days with true success. Because of Jesus, we have constant access to the throne of almighty God to ask Him for help and hope—at any moment in every single circumstance.

Dear Jesus, thank You for understanding my weakness. I'm so glad I can come to You and receive what I don't have on my own—real, everlasting strength and courage and confidence and power.

Have the Guts to Forgive—a Lot!

[Jesus said,] "For if you forgive other people when they sin against you, your heavenly Father will also forgive you. But if you do not forgive others their sins, your Father will not forgive your sins."
MATTHEW 6:14–15 NIV

Has someone hurt you or made you mad recently? How did you feel about forgiving that person? It's not easy. Sometimes we're just annoyed with others and need to forgive them so we don't stay annoyed. The Bible is clear that our willingness to forgive is a really big deal. Jesus said that God won't forgive our sins if we don't forgive others. And who doesn't need the Lord to forgive her mistakes? We all do, every day. When we're upset with someone who treated us badly, we have to think of how much we need forgiveness for the things we do wrong too. Jesus forgives generously—He died on the cross so our sins could be forgiven!—and we should want to offer forgiveness generously as well.

Dear Jesus, when I struggle to forgive, remind me of how thankful I am that You forgive my sins. I want to be like You. Amen.

Jonah Learned the Hard Way

Jonah was in the belly of the fish three days and three nights.
JONAH 1:17 ESV

Take some time to read about Jonah in the Bible. His story is an example of what can happen when God asks us to be gutsy and brave for a specific task and we don't listen. Jonah didn't want to go to Nineveh and preach there like God asked him to do, so he made his own plan and sailed in the opposite direction. But God sent such a strong storm that the boat Jonah was sailing on nearly broke apart—until the sailors threw Jonah into the sea. Then a large fish swallowed Jonah and kept him in its belly for three days. While he sat in that fish's belly, Jonah prayed and worshipped God. Then God told the fish to spit Jonah out onto dry land. Eventually Jonah did obey God and go to Nineveh, but he should have listened the first time!

Dear God, let me remember Jonah when I'm tempted to do my own thing instead of obeying You. Help me to obey Your commands and remember that there can be bad consequences if I don't. Help me not to have to learn things the hard way. Amen.

Online and Offline

I will set no sinful thing in front of my eyes.
PSALM 101:3 NLV

Pretty much everyone spends *huge* amounts of time online and on a cell phone these days. Having access to so much information and so many ways to interact with people can be awesome, but there is a whole lot of junk and evil online too. You constantly need to ask God for wisdom and establish healthy guidelines and boundaries for time spent online. You need to have accountability. We all do—because we're all sinners and can easily and quickly get caught up in stuff that's no good for us and can even destroy us.

You also need to have courage to stand strong against any friends pressuring you to spend time online in ways you know are wrong or have been told are off-limits or dangerous by parents and good leaders in your life. This can be hard, especially when it seems like others have no limits online. But be gutsy about it. Don't cave to the peer pressure. Let God help you, and watch Him bless you when you remain brave and strong.

Dear God, please help me to set limits and stay away from unhealthy and sinful things online. The world is connected through the internet, but I need to disconnect in healthy ways too. Please give me wisdom and self-control, both online and offline. Amen.

God Knows Absolutely Everything

*O LORD, you have examined my heart and know everything about me.
You know when I sit down or stand up. You know my thoughts even when
I'm far away. You see me when I travel and when I rest at home. You know
everything I do. You know what I am going to say even before I say it, LORD.
You go before me and follow me. You place your hand of blessing on my head.
Such knowledge is too wonderful for me, too great for me to understand!*
PSALM 139:1–6 NLT

God knows absolutely everything about you—every move, every word,
every choice, every thought. You have nothing to worry about if you love
God and are letting the Holy Spirit lead your life. Take comfort in knowing
that God sees and knows all. That truth should make you gutsy and brave.
Because God knows all about you, He can care for you, protect you, teach
you, and love you in all the best ways, like no one else possibly can.

**Dear God, You know absolutely everything—including every single
thing about me—and You love me and care for me and lead me
through life. I'm amazed and grateful! Thank You! Amen.**

Stay Alert!

Stay alert! Watch out for your great enemy, the devil. He prowls around like a roaring lion, looking for someone to devour. Stand firm against him, and be strong in your faith. Remember that your family of believers all over the world is going through the same kind of suffering you are.

1 PETER 5:8–9 NLT

To really be gutsy doesn't mean you pretend there's nothing to be worried about or afraid of. This scripture shares the hard truth that Christians definitely have an enemy—the devil, also known as Satan—who is like a lion wanting to destroy us. We need to be aware of him and have courage to stand against and fight him. And how do we do that? By staying close to God. We have to read His Word, pray constantly, and be involved in a Bible-teaching church that helps us grow closer to God. We have to pursue friendships with people who encourage and support us in our faith and set boundaries between ourselves and those who try to lead us away from God. The devil wants to destroy us by isolating us or by providing friends who are bad influences on us. He will try to tempt us to disobey and reject God and His Word. But we can stand up to the devil and fight with the power of the Holy Spirit within us!

Dear God, please help me to stay alert to the devil's schemes and be ready to fight him in Your power. Amen.

Jesus Gives You Perfect Peace

[Jesus said,] "The Advocate, the Holy Spirit, whom the Father will send in my name, will teach you all things and will remind you of everything I have said to you. Peace I leave with you; my peace I give you. I do not give to you as the world gives. Do not let your hearts be troubled and do not be afraid."

JOHN 14:26–27 NIV

Jesus said these words to His disciples, and they are for you today too. Jesus gives you supernatural peace. Peaceful things here on earth—a relaxing beach, a quiet afternoon, a nice time with family and friends—sure are wonderful and refreshing, but they are not the deep, continuous, miraculous peace that only Jesus can give. Whenever you feel anxious or afraid, let the Holy Spirit help you remember the perfect peace of Jesus.

Dear Jesus, anytime I'm troubled or afraid, please calm me down and quiet my mind and heart through Your Holy Spirit within me. Remind me constantly of Your perfect peace. Amen.

Gutsy When Facing Mean Girls

*"Be strong and courageous. Do not be afraid or terrified
because of them, for the LORD your God goes with you;
he will never leave you nor forsake you."*
DEUTERONOMY 31:6 NIV

Have you ever had to deal with mean girls—selfish girls who are always looking for conflict and causing trouble and creating drama and hurting others? Girls like that can make life miserable, and you need a lot of gutsiness to keep on going when facing them. Be sure to pray *a lot* for wisdom on how to handle situations with mean girls. Maybe you'll have to work on projects at school together, or maybe you'll need to stick up for a friend mean girls are picking on. Or maybe you'll be the one being hurt by them. Whatever the case, God will give you wisdom and help when you ask. Pray for the hearts of the mean girls too. Read and remember what God says about loving enemies (Matthew 5:43–48; Luke 6:27–31; Romans 12:20–21, for example). Pray for them to be dramatically changed by the love of God and for them to see God's love through you!

**Dear God, help me to be gutsy when facing mean girls,
and give me wisdom for interacting with them. Please
turn their hearts toward You and Your love. Amen.**

Superpower

God gave us a spirit not of fear but of power and love and self-control.
2 TIMOTHY 1:7 ESV

If you were given a superpower, what power would you want? And if you got it, would you want to sit around and never use it? Of course not! Now think about how God has given you His superpower through the Holy Spirit in you. He has given you a spirit of power and love and self-control to defeat any spirit of fear. You don't just want to sit around doing nothing with that, do you? Ask God every day what brave and gutsy things He wants to do through you! How does He want you to share with and serve people? How does He want you to spread His truth and encouragement and love?

Dear God, in a way, You truly have given me a superpower because You are in me through Your Holy Spirit. I want to live for You and serve You with all the good gifts and talents You have given me. Show me each day the things You want me to do, all to give You praise! Amen.

Don't Be the Boss

If your sinful old self is the boss over your mind, it leads to death.
But if the Holy Spirit is the boss over your mind, it leads to life and peace.
The mind that thinks only of ways to please the sinful old self is fighting
against God. It is not able to obey God's Laws. It never can. Those who
do what their sinful old selves want to do cannot please God. But you are
not doing what your sinful old selves want you to do. You are doing what
the Holy Spirit tells you to do, if you have God's Spirit living in you.
ROMANS 8:6–9 NLV

A gutsy girl often wants to be the boss. But wanting to be your own boss is actually a bad idea! The Bible says that having your sinful self as your boss will lead to death. But having God's Holy Spirit as your boss will lead to life and peace. He wants to "boss" you in the best kind of ways to lead you to the very best blessings.

Dear God, please help me not to want to be my own boss but to let Your Holy Spirit guide and direct me in everything I do. Amen.

It's Gutsy Just to Cry Sometimes

Then Jesus cried.
JOHN 11:35 NLV

Do you ever feel like crying and you're not even sure why? Sometimes it's because of frustration or sadness, and it's actually gutsy just to stop and give yourself time and space to feel those emotions and give them to God as you pray to Him. If you bottle up your emotions instead of releasing them, they'll often explode in other ways or make you feel sick inside. So don't ever think that crying means you're a pathetic wimp. Listening to your emotions, figuring out where they're coming from, and allowing yourself time and space to release them actually takes a lot of courage. When you can name your emotions and recognize their source, they don't have to scare you or make you act out in ways that might lead you down bad paths and get you into trouble. Sharing your emotions with God and your family, friends, and mentors is one of the very best ways to deal with them.

> Dear God, give me peace about letting myself cry when I need to. Help me to listen to my emotions and figure out how to handle them in healthy ways. Please also point me to the best people to talk to about my emotions, those who will guide me with Your truth and wisdom. Amen.

The Midwives Were Gutsy

*Because the midwives feared God, they refused to obey
the king's orders. They allowed the boys to live.*
EXODUS 1:17 NLT

Shiphrah and Puah were two really gutsy women in the Bible. During the time when God's people, the Israelites, lived in Egypt, the pharaoh decided there were too many of them. He was afraid the Israelites would join together and conspire to take away his power. So he made all the Israelites slaves, and he made sure they were treated cruelly. The pharaoh even ordered that every new baby boy born to an Israelite mother must be killed. But two midwives (those who helped new moms as they delivered their babies) named Shiphrah and Puah respected God and secretly refused to kill babies. God blessed them for their great courage. And because of it, the man who would lead the Israelites out of Egypt—Moses—was safely born to his mother, Jochebed.

*Dear God, thank You for Your Word and the example in it of
Shiphrah and Puah, who were gutsy enough to defy an evil
king to save the lives of many of Your people. Please give me
wisdom and courage like these midwives had. Amen.*

We Need Each Other

First of all, I keep thanking my God, through Jesus Christ, for all of you. This is because the whole world knows of your faith in Christ. God knows how I work for Him. He knows how I preach with all my heart the Good News about His Son. He knows how I always pray for you. I pray that I might be able to visit you, if God wants me to. I want to see you so I can share some special gift of the Holy Spirit with you. It will make you strong. Both of us need help. I can help make your faith strong and you can do the same for me. We need each other.

ROMANS 1:8–12 NLV

Do you feel grateful for your family and friends who also boldly follow Jesus? You totally should! We all need one another because together we are stronger. We encourage one another by sharing the gifts we've received from the Holy Spirit, by sharing the ways God is working in our lives, and by sharing truth from the Bible with one another. And we get to have fun spending time together and worshipping God together too!

Dear God, thank You for the family and friends in my life who help make my faith in You stronger and bolder. Help me to encourage them and make them stronger and bolder too. Amen.

Know Exactly Who You Are

God created man in his own image, in the image of God
he created him; male and female he created them.
GENESIS 1:27 ESV

More and more people these days seem so sadly lost, trying to find their identities. We can be strong and confident in our own identities and help others be strong too. All we need to do is consistently look to God, the one true Creator! His Word is clear in Genesis 1 that God made people in His likeness. He has made boys to grow up into men and girls to grow up into women—all with unique and awesome traits and personalities—and He has given us the Bible to guide us in how to live and love like He does. When people choose to accept Jesus as Savior, they become new creations. They can say, "Christ lives in me. The life I now live in this body, I live by putting my trust in the Son of God. He was the One Who loved me and gave Himself for me" (Galatians 2:20 NLV).

Heavenly Father, I'm so thankful You created me with purpose and that I can say, "Christ lives in me!" I know who I am. I am Your child, and I live my life for Jesus. Please help me to be strong and bold about sharing the truth and goodness of Your Word with others. Amen.

Stand Against Sin

Well then, should we keep on sinning so that God can show
us more and more of his wonderful grace? Of course not!
ROMANS 6:1–2 NLT

Lots of people think it's no big deal to sin—to make bad choices and disobey God's Word. They just want to do what everyone else in the world says is popular and fun. And they might think that since Jesus saves people from sin, then why not sin however much you want and not worry about it?

But no matter how much love and forgiveness God gives, sin always has consequences. So anyone who claims to be a Christian but doesn't attempt to obey God will certainly have a lot of trouble.

Don't misunderstand—doing your best to obey God's Word doesn't mean you'll have a perfect life with no trouble. But it does mean that God will help you through every trouble and work everything out for good for those who love Him (Romans 8:28). So be gutsy and refuse to follow along with the world's popular ideas that sinning is fun and that God and His Word are just killjoys. God will bless and reward you for committing yourself to Him in love and for doing your best to avoid sin as His Word instructs (Romans 6:11–14; 2 Timothy 2:22).

Dear God, please help me stand against sin.
I want to stay committed to loving and
following You and Your perfect ways. Amen.

God Reaches Out His Hand

Though the LORD is great, he cares for the humble, but he keeps his distance from the proud. Though I am surrounded by troubles, you will protect me from the anger of my enemies. You reach out your hand, and the power of your right hand saves me. The LORD will work out his plans for my life—for your faithful love, O LORD, endures forever. Don't abandon me, for you made me.
PSALM 138:6–8 NLT

Have you ever felt like someone truly hated you? Maybe someone was making your life miserable and you knew it was on purpose. In tough situations like that, focus on this scripture. God can reach out His hand to protect you from the anger or hatefulness of anyone who might want to harm you. He sees your enemies and won't let them defeat you. Keep calling out and depending on Him, and then praise Him as you see His hand reaching out to protect and help you.

Dear God, I feel hated by _____ , and I'm overwhelmed. Please reach out Your hand to protect and save me. Show me Your love and kindness and justice, and work out Your perfect plans for my life. I trust in Your faithful love and care. Amen.

Joshua and Caleb Were Gutsy

[Joshua and Caleb] said to all the people of Israel, . . . "If the Lord is pleased with us, then He will bring us into this land and give it to us. It is a land which flows with milk and honey. Only do not go against the Lord. And do not be afraid of the people of the land."
NUMBERS 14:7–9 NLV

God had said to Moses that one day He was going to give the land of Canaan to His people. So Moses sent Joshua, Caleb, and ten other men to spy on the land for forty days. When they returned, they reported that Canaan was wonderful, but the people were powerful and the cities well protected. This news didn't scare Joshua and Caleb, for they were confident that God would help them take over the land of Canaan. But ten of the spies were scared. Then those ten men spread so much fear among the people of Israel that the people rebelled and complained against their leaders, Moses and Aaron. God grew angry with the Israelites because they listened to fear rather than listening to the courage and faith of Joshua and Caleb.

Dear God, help me to be gutsy like Joshua and Caleb. Help me not to listen to fears that say You are not powerful enough to work out Your good plans. I trust in You, and I know You can accomplish anything! Amen.

Know How Awesome You Are

*See what great love the Father has for us that He would call
us His children. And that is what we are. For this reason the
people of the world do not know who we are because they did
not know Him. Dear friends, we are God's children now.*

1 JOHN 3:1–2 NLV

Sometimes we feel hopeless, discouraged, and anything but gutsy and brave.
Can you relate? It might be because you've forgotten who you are. In times
like that you especially need to go to scripture and remind yourself of these
awesome truths:

- You are made in the image of God (Genesis 1:26).

- You are wonderfully made (Psalm 139:14).

- You are God's masterpiece (Ephesians 2:10).

- When you accept Jesus as your Savior, you become a child of God
  and are filled with the powerful Holy Spirit (John 1:12; Romans 8:11).

- You are royalty (1 Peter 2:9).

**Dear God, help me not to forget who I am. I am Your child, and You
are my heavenly Father who created me on purpose, and You love me
unconditionally. Thank You! I'm holding on to You and never want to let
go. Please lead and guide me on the paths You have planned for me.**

Use Your Gifts for God

*In his grace, God has given us different
gifts for doing certain things well.*
ROMANS 12:6 NLT

Are you using your talents and abilities to bring glory to God? Don't ever forget that He gave them to you. First Corinthians 12:4–7 (NLV) says, "There are different kinds of gifts. But it is the same Holy Spirit Who gives them. There are different kinds of work to be done for Him. But the work is for the same Lord. There are different ways of doing His work. But it is the same God who uses all these ways in all people. The Holy Spirit works in each person in one way or another for the good of all."

It's easy to look around at other people's gifts and talents and wish we had them instead of our own. But we need to fight that urge to compare and be jealous. We need to ask God for contentment and joy in our own unique abilities. He will show us the ways He wants to use them to help and bless others, all while bringing Him glory and pointing others to Him!

> Dear God, please help me to realize the good gifts of the natural abilities You've given me. Help me not to compare myself to others. I want to look to You alone and be happy and grateful for my own skills and talents—and use them to worship You and help others to love You too. Amen.

When You Just Want to Quit

*I have learned the secret of living in every situation, whether it
is with a full stomach or empty, with plenty or little. For I can
do everything through Christ, who gives me strength.*
PHILIPPIANS 4:12–13 NLT

Have you ever wanted to quit something? Maybe you wished you could drop out of a class at school because it felt way too hard. Or maybe you tried a new sport but didn't want to finish the season. We've all been there. But have you ever stuck something out and then looked back to see how God was giving you courage and strength to take things one day at a time? Do you feel like you've grown into a better, stronger person because you endured instead of quitting?

In any hard situation, if we call on God to help and then trust and wait on Him, He will either help us walk through it day by day until it's over or help us find a wise way out immediately. It takes gutsiness to depend on God's strength, wait on His perfect timing, and let Him help us persevere instead of just giving up.

**Dear God, I don't want to quit. Please help
me persevere when I need to. Amen.**

Jochebed Was Gutsy

When she could hide him no longer, she got a papyrus basket for him. . . . Then she placed the child in it and put it among the reeds along the bank of the Nile.

EXODUS 2:3 NIV

As Jochebed's infant son grew, he became too big to hide from Pharaoh's evil plan to kill all Hebrew baby boys. So Jochebed placed him inside a waterproof basket and put it among the reeds near the edge of the Nile River. She knew that Pharaoh's daughter often came there. Soon the princess found the baby crying and felt sorry for him and wanted him for her own son. His sister Miriam offered to find a mother who could feed him until he could eat regular food, and the princess agreed that Jochebed should take care of the baby for a while longer. She had no idea she was talking to the baby's real mother! But God knew.

Jochebed was thrilled to spend more time with her son. And then when baby Moses grew old enough, Jochebed gave him back to Pharaoh's daughter. Jochebed must have ached when she had to give up her son, but more important than her feelings was protecting her child and obeying God's good plans. Because of his mother's courage, Moses was saved from Pharaoh's evil plans and grew to be one of God's greatest leaders of all time.

Dear God, thank You for showing me the gutsiness of Jochebed in Your Word. Help me to learn from her example. Amen.

David Was Gutsy

Goliath, the Philistine champion from Gath, came out from the Philistine ranks. Then David heard him shout his usual taunt to the army of Israel.

1 SAMUEL 17:23 NLT

Take some time to read about David and Goliath in the Bible. Even though he was younger and smaller than many others in the army of Israel, David knew God had helped him fight lions and bears in the past, and so God would help him fight the Philistine giant everyone else was afraid of. David said, "You come to me with sword and spear to kill me, but I come to you in the name of the Lord Almighty, the God of Israel. You have defied Him, but today He will conquer you! Everyone here will know that the Lord rescues His people—but not with sword and spear. This is God's battle, and He will give you to us!" (see 1 Samuel 17:45–47).

Let David's gutsy example inspire you! Sometimes you simply need to remember all the ways God has helped you fight and win in the past—and that can give you all the peace and courage you need to let God help you win whatever battle is in front of you right now.

Almighty God, help me to have fearless confidence in You and Your power and protection—just like David did! Amen.

A Gutsy Friendship

There was an immediate bond between them, for Jonathan loved David.
1 SAMUEL 18:1 NLT

After David bravely killed the giant Goliath, Saul, who was king of Israel, was impressed. So King Saul summoned David to work for him, and David soon met the king's son, Jonathan. These two guys quickly bonded. Jonathan loved David and promised to be his loyal friend forever.

Since David was so brave, King Saul wanted David to lead his armies. And because God was with him, David was hugely successful. But then one day King Saul grew jealous, believing that the people of Israel respected David more than they respected him. The king grew so jealous that he actually wanted to kill David. He told all his servants and even his son Jonathan to kill David. But Jonathan could never do that. Instead, he warned David about the king's orders. Jonathan helped protect David and stayed loyal to his friend no matter what. Jonathan could have become jealous of David. He could have wanted to become the next king after Saul instead of David. But Jonathan truly loved God and truly loved his friend David.

**Dear God, please help me to be the kind of gutsy
friend Jonathan was—courageous and loyal and
loving and selfless no matter what. Amen.**

King of All Kings, Lord of All Lords

*At just the right time Christ will be revealed from heaven by the
blessed and only almighty God, the King of all kings and Lord of
all lords. He alone can never die, and he lives in light so brilliant
that no human can approach him. No human eye has ever seen
him, nor ever will. All honor and power to him forever! Amen.*

1 TIMOTHY 6:15–16 NLT

Imagine if you could pick up the phone and call the richest and most powerful politicians, royalty, and leaders in the world anytime you wanted. You would feel brave knowing that they could come to your rescue for anything you needed. Not many of us are going to have close connections with important leaders, but that doesn't matter—because we *do* have a close connection and instant communication with the highest King of all time—our one true God who is above all! And because of Jesus, we can approach His throne and ask for His help with anything at any time (Hebrews 4:16). Wow! That should make us feel gutsy and ready to face anything.

**Dear God, You are the highest and best and most powerful
of all, and yet You love me and want to help me. I am
amazed and thankful, and I love You too! Amen.**

Think About Sandcastles

*[Jesus said,] "Everyone who hears these words of mine and does not
do them will be like a foolish man who built his house on the sand.
And the rain fell, and the floods came, and the winds blew and beat
against that house, and it fell, and great was the fall of it."*

MATTHEW 7:26–27 ESV

Have you ever watched sandcastle artists? Not just kids at the beach, but
the professional artists? They're amazing! But no matter their talent, a
sandcastle never lasts for too long in the waves and weather. Jesus warned
about building our spiritual houses on sand: Any person building on sand
(the things of this world that will pass away) will never find true security. But
any person building on the strong foundation of the rock of Jesus and His
Word will stand firm and brave through all kinds of tough situations. Jesus
was comparing people who hear His teaching and obey it to people who
only listen to it but do nothing with it. Those who listen and obey Jesus are
built up strong to endure whatever life brings their way, while those who
ignore Jesus are easily washed away.

**Dear Jesus, I don't want to ignore You and let my faith in you be easily
washed away! Please build me up on Your Word to be gutsy and
strong for my whole life because I know and truly live for You. Amen.**

Don't Dwell on Fears

You are standing under the powerful hand of God. At the right time He will lift you up. Give all your worries to Him because He cares for you.
1 PETER 5:6–7 NLV

When we have scary experiences, we naturally want to avoid the possibility of anything similar happening again. If you've been attacked by a dog once, you might never want to be anywhere near dogs again. But would that mean never going to a public park or beach or place where dogs often are—or the house of any friend who has a dog? Living in fear like that wouldn't be healthy or fun. It's best to work through fears created from our experiences and not let them overcome us or keep us from doing good things.

Depending on what our fears are, sometimes we can work through them with help from family and friends, and sometimes we need extra help, like seeing a good counselor for therapy. God is always able to provide exactly the comfort and the people and the resources we need to help us with anxiety and fear. We only have to ask Him and trust Him to lead!

Dear God, thank You for caring about my fears. Please help me to work through them and learn from them rather than run away from and avoid them. Give me comfort and wisdom and provide everything I need, including the right people and resources, to overcome every fear. Amen.

God Never Gets Tired of Your Prayers

You must pray at all times as the Holy Spirit leads
you to pray. Pray for the things that are needed.
You must watch and keep on praying.
EPHESIANS 6:18 NLV

Some gutsy girls get told they talk too much. But guess what? No girl can ever talk too much to God. He will never, ever get tired of hearing from you in prayer. The Bible says to pray "at all times as the Holy Spirit leads you." And also "Never stop praying. In everything give thanks" (1 Thessalonians 5:17–18 NLV). Pray to your loving heavenly Father, and praise Him in your mind every moment of every day—and especially as the Holy Spirit leads you. Ask Him for His help and wisdom for yourself and for others in all situations. Worship Him and thank Him for who He is and for what He does. Tell Him about the needs of others and your own needs. Let Him be your most trusted listening ear and your constant best friend.

Dear God, help me to remember I can never talk to You too much.
I can pray to You at all times—no matter what time it is, where
I am, or who I'm with. Thank You for loving me and wanting
to lead me and help me in every aspect of my life. Amen.

Abigail Was Gutsy

She was an intelligent and beautiful woman,
but her husband was surly and mean in his dealings.
1 SAMUEL 25:3 NIV

Take some time to read Abigail's story in the Bible. Not long before David became king of Israel, there was a man named Nabal who was very rich. His wife's name was Abigail, and she was kind and wise. But Nabal was foolish and sinful. In the past, David had helped protect the men who worked for Nabal. When David and his men set up camp near where Nabal and his men were working, David sent some of his men to go to Nabal to ask him for food and supplies. David had been kind to Nabal's men, so he figured Nabal would be kind in return. But Nabal refused to help and made David so angry that he was ready to fight and kill.

One of Nabal's men went to Abigail to tell her what had happened. Right away she sent food and drink to David and his men. When Abigail met up with them, she begged David not to be angry and vengeful toward Nabal's men because of Nabal's selfishness. David listened to her and thanked her. Nabal acted in foolishness, and David nearly overreacted in great anger. But Abigail acted with calm, cool wisdom and generosity, and she saved many people's lives.

Dear God, let Abigail's gutsiness inspire me. Help me to
be a wise and generous peacemaker too. Amen.

Immortal, Invisible, the Only God

To the King of the ages, immortal, invisible,
the only God, be honor and glory forever and ever.
1 TIMOTHY 1:17 ESV

Did you ever have an imaginary friend when you were a little girl, an invisible pal to play games and be silly with? As you grew older, you outgrew that "friend," but technically you actually do still have an invisible friend—though He is not imaginary or silly at all! The Bible talks about God being invisible, and Hebrews 11:27 specifically tells us that as Moses led God's people out of Egypt, he did not fear Pharaoh because he kept his eyes on our invisible God. The Bible also tells us to fix our eyes not on what we can see but on what we can't see (2 Corinthians 4:18). Real gutsiness and courage come from real faith that God is who He says He is and loves and protects us even though we can't see Him with our human vision.

Dear God, You might be invisible to my human eyes, but You are not imaginary. I have seen and felt You working in my life, protecting me and loving me and providing for me. Please keep showing me more and keep growing my faith in You! Amen.

A Young Servant Girl Was Gutsy

Naaman the captain of the army of the king of Syria was an important man to his king. He was much respected, . . .but he had a bad skin disease. Now the Syrians had gone out in groups of soldiers, and had taken a little girl from the land of Israel. She served Naaman's wife. And she said to her owner, "I wish that my owner's husband were with the man of God who is in Samaria! Then he would heal his bad skin disease."

2 KINGS 5:1–3 NLV

You would think a respected and important army captain might not listen to a simple young servant girl from Israel, but Naaman did. Because of what she said, he was willing to go to the man Elisha, a prophet of the one true God, to see if his bad skin disease could be healed. If you read the whole story, you will find that Naaman was healed, and then he believed in God alone! The servant girl was gutsy to speak up and share her faith in God. She trusted that He had the true power to heal through His prophet Elisha.

Dear God, I want to be inspired by the young servant girl who spoke up to share her faith with Naaman. Thank You for showing Your healing power and bringing more people to great faith in You! Amen.

Encouragement

Encourage one another and build one another up.
1 Thessalonians 5:11 ESV

Think of a time when you really needed some extra encouragement and then you got it. What happened? Did you get a gift from a friend "just because"? Maybe your parents treated you to something special and totally unexpected. Maybe a teacher noticed how hard you worked on a project and celebrated with you in class. Or maybe it was just a simple smile that was contagious right when you needed it. Whatever it was, think of how it made you feel. Encouragement fills you with joy and confidence. Also, don't miss that the word *courage* is in the word *encouragement*. When someone encourages you, that person helps you feel brave and gutsy too—ready to face anything because you know you have people in your life who love and care about you and will always support you and cheer you on.

So next time you encourage someone in even the simplest way, and when you receive any kind of encouragement, think about how it's not just to spread joy but to help others have courage in the midst of any problem or hardship or worry or fear.

Dear God, thank You for the wonderful people who encourage me so well. Help me to be an awesome encourager too. Amen.

How Not to Worry

*[Jesus said,] "That is why I tell you not to worry about everyday life—
whether you have enough food and drink, or enough clothes to wear.
Isn't life more than food, and your body more than clothing? Look at
the birds. They don't plant or harvest or store food in barns, for your
heavenly Father feeds them. And aren't you far more valuable to him than
they are? Can all your worries add a single moment to your life?"*
MATTHEW 6:25–27 NLT

Jesus made it clear that we're not supposed to worry. But it's easy to read these verses, do our best not to worry for a while, and then get right back to worrying again anyway. So what can we do? This passage goes on to tell us to seek God's kingdom first (Matthew 6:31–33). If we're focused on Him and what He wants us to do, then we won't have time for worries. How can we seek God's kingdom first? We can begin each day by talking to Him. We can read the Bible and learn the good things He has for us. We can do our best in all our work and relationships. We can root out and confess sin in our lives. We can especially look for ways to love others like Jesus loves. When we focus on those things, we won't have time or brain space for worries to creep in!

**Dear Jesus, help me to focus on You and Your
kingdom first and foremost! Amen.**

Three Gutsy Guys

*"If we are thrown into the blazing furnace,
the God whom we serve is able to save us."*
Daniel 3:17 NLT

Take some time to read about Shadrach, Meshach, and Abednego in the Bible. These three gutsy guys refused to worship anyone but the one true God. And King Nebuchadnezzar was furious. He had ordered everyone in his kingdom to worship a gold statue, and if they would not, they were to be thrown into a fiery furnace. But Shadrach, Meshach, and Abednego bravely said, "If you throw us into the fiery furnace, the God we serve is able to save us from it. But even if He does not, we will *never* serve your gods."

The angry king ordered the furnace to be heated seven times hotter than normal and commanded his soldiers to tie up Shadrach, Meshach, and Abednego and throw them into the fire. As King Nebuchadnezzar watched, suddenly he leaped to his feet. "Look!" he said. "I see *four* men walking around in the fire, untied and unharmed, and the fourth man looks like a god!" (see Daniel 3:25). So he called for the men to come out of the fire—and not even a hair on their heads was burned, and they didn't even smell like fire! God had protected and rescued the gutsy guys who were faithful to Him.

**Dear God, Shadrach, Meshach, and Abednego knew that
even dying for You was better than worshipping a false god.
Help me to remember their faithful example. Amen.**

Be Strong and Very Courageous

"Be strong and very courageous, being careful to do according to all the law that Moses my servant commanded you. Do not turn from it to the right hand or to the left, that you may have good success wherever you go. This Book of the Law shall not depart from your mouth, but you shall meditate on it day and night, so that you may be careful to do according to all that is written in it. For then you will make your way prosperous, and then you will have good success. Have I not commanded you? Be strong and courageous. Do not be frightened, and do not be dismayed, for the LORD your God is with you wherever you go."

JOSHUA 1:7–9 ESV

God called Joshua to be the one who would lead His people into the promised land after wandering in the desert for forty years. In Joshua 1 you can read what God said to Joshua to help him be the brave new leader. God's words aren't just for Joshua though. You can let this scripture help you be gutsy too. You can let God powerfully encourage and embolden you as He leads you into the wonderful purposes He has for your life!

Dear God, thank You for Your powerful words of encouragement to Joshua long ago—and that I can be strengthened and motivated by those same words even today. Amen.

Strength, Rock, Fortress, Savior. . .

I love you, LORD; you are my strength. The LORD is my rock, my fortress, and my savior; my God is my rock, in whom I find protection. He is my shield, the power that saves me, and my place of safety. I called on the LORD, who is worthy of praise, and he saved me from my enemies. The ropes of death entangled me; floods of destruction swept over me. The grave wrapped its ropes around me; death laid a trap in my path. But in my distress I cried out to the LORD; yes, I prayed to my God for help. He heard me from his sanctuary; my cry to him reached his ears.

PSALM 18:1–6 NLT

Focusing on and memorizing scripture is one of the best ways ever to develop your gutsiness! Even if you just memorize verse 1 of Psalm 18, you have a simple but powerful prayer to God for any kind of challenge or trouble. And if you go on to memorize verse 2, the passage will remind you that God is your

- strength,
- rock,
- fortress,
- Savior,
- shield,
- power, and
- place of safety.

Dear God, I want to love and learn Your Word. Help me to memorize it. Fill up my brain with awesome power from scripture so I can force out worry and fear. Amen.

With Jesus, You Can Overcome

You, dear children, are from God and have overcome them,
because the one who is in you is greater than the one who is in the
world. They are from the world and therefore speak from the viewpoint
of the world, and the world listens to them. We are from God.

1 JOHN 4:4–6 NIV

Everyone has at least a few fears and worries. There's no use pretending we don't. And being truly gutsy means admitting fears and worries and facing them head-on. You can't be gutsy unless you first know that you're scared of something but then deal with it. And sometimes you'll deal with things so well that you totally overcome them so that they are never a problem again! With God's Holy Spirit working in you to help, you can face anything and triumph over it. Jesus said, "I have told you these things, so that in me you may have peace. In this world you will have trouble. But take heart! I have overcome the world" (John 16:33 NIV).

Dear God, I don't want to deny my fears and worries. I want to admit and face them, knowing how much I need Your help with them. I believe wholeheartedly that You can help me overcome anything, according to Your will. Amen.

Rahab Was Gutsy

[Joshua] said to them, "Go and spy out the land, and Jericho."
So they went and came to the house of Rahab.

JOSHUA 2:1 NLV

Rahab was a woman in the Bible who helped two men Joshua had sent into the land of Canaan to spy on the city of Jericho. The men came to her house, but then someone warned the king that they were spies. So Rahab hid the two spies on the roof of her home. She told them that she trusted in their God and asked them to protect her family when they came into the land of Canaan to take it over. The spies promised to protect Rahab and her family as long as she didn't tell anyone about their plans. Then Rahab let them down by a rope through the window and told them to hide for three days in the hill country before returning home. Later, by that same red rope, the spies knew where to find her and her family to protect them when the Israelites took over Jericho. The Israelite spies had needed help, and God prompted Rahab to believe in Him and have courage to hide the spies at exactly the right time.

Dear God, please make me gutsy like Rahab, and remind me that You provide exactly the right help through exactly the right people at exactly the right time. Amen.

You're Weak—God's Not

Christ is not weak when He works in your hearts. He uses His power in you. Christ's weak human body died on a cross. It is by God's power that Christ lives today. We are weak. We are as He was. But we will be alive with Christ through the power God has for us.
2 Corinthians 13:3–4 NLV

What's exhausting you these days? Just admit it! It's okay to feel tired and need rest! Don't ever get down on yourself for feeling weak and weary. The truth is that you *are* weak as a human being. We all are. There's no use denying it. But God is not weak. Remember that with the Holy Spirit in you, you have the same power that raised Jesus from death to life working in you (Romans 8:11). That's incredible! Whatever God has planned for you to do in life, you can trust that you will not be endlessly weak. He will give you the gifts and strengths and tools you need at exactly the right times. Day by day, simply live for Him and find rest in Him faithfully, just as His Word instructs. And someday God's power in you will enable you to live forever in heaven too.

Dear God, thank You that You are never weak.
You make me strong with Your unfailing power.
I will keep following and depending on You! Amen.

Ruth Was Gutsy

Ruth replied, "Don't ask me to leave you and turn back."
RUTH 1:16 NLT

Take some time to read about Ruth in the Bible. Ruth, her mother-in-law, Naomi, and her sister-in-law, Orpah, were left alone when their husbands all died. And life was really bad for single women back then.

Naomi told Ruth and Orpah to leave her and go back to their old homes since they were still young and could find new husbands. So Orpah decided to leave, but Ruth refused. She clung to Naomi, saying, "I want to go where you go. I want to stay where you stay. I want your people to be my people. I want your God to be my God. I never want to leave you as long as I am alive."

When Naomi realized Ruth's loyalty and love, she stopped pushing her to go. The two traveled together back to Bethlehem. There God blessed Ruth as she worked picking up leftover grain in the fields. God led her to a good man named Boaz. When he heard about Ruth's loyalty and love for her mother-in-law, he was impressed, and he admired her. He protected and provided for Ruth and Naomi and grew to love Ruth, taking her as his wife.

Dear God, please give me a gutsy loyalty to my loved ones like Ruth had, even during hard times. Help me to look out not only for myself but for others too. I believe You will bless me for showing true loyalty and love. Amen.

Gutsy Because of God's Word

*Every word of God proves true. He is a shield
to all who come to him for protection.*
PROVERBS 30:5 NLT

Memorizing scripture will help you be a gutsy girl. Scripture is a powerful tool and weapon against anxiety and fear. God loves to bring verses to your mind exactly when you need them. Sometimes repeating the most calming scriptures, like Psalm 23, in your mind can help you to relax your breathing and racing thoughts when you feel panicky. Sometimes singing praises like those in Psalm 136 is exactly what you need to have joy and get rid of the fear creeping in on you. Sometimes powerful scriptures that recount the faith of others and the miracles of God, like Hebrews 11, are exactly what you need to grow your faith, helping you trust that God can do any kind of miracle in your situation too. Keep filling your mind with God's Word every chance you get. Memorize it and see how God uses it to guide you, care for you, and protect you.

Dear God, thank You for Your powerful Word. Please help me to memorize a lot of it. Bring specific verses to my mind exactly when I need them to keep my mind fixed on You and Your power! Amen.

Your Help Comes from the Lord

I will lift up my eyes to the mountains. Where will my help come from?
My help comes from the Lord, Who made heaven and earth. He will not let
your feet go out from under you. He Who watches over you will not sleep.
Listen, He Who watches over Israel will not close his eyes or sleep. The Lord
watches over you. The Lord is your safe cover at your right hand. The sun
will not hurt you during the day and the moon will not hurt you during the
night. The Lord will keep you from all that is sinful. He will watch over your
soul. The Lord will watch over your coming and going, now and forever.
PSALM 121 NLV

When you read Psalm 121, how can you not feel gutsy? The almighty God of
the universe promises you amazing, endless help and protection. He never
sleeps and never stops watching out for you. No one else offers the kind of
love and peace and security that He does. Spend some time focusing on
this psalm and praising God for His awesome love and care for you.

Dear God, I praise You for Your love, protection, and care!
You are awesome and mighty, and I have nothing to fear.
Thank You for watching over me so well. Amen.

Missionaries Are Gutsy

[Jesus] replied, "The Father alone has the authority to set those dates and times, and they are not for you to know. But you will receive power when the Holy Spirit comes upon you. And you will be my witnesses, telling people about me everywhere—in Jerusalem, throughout Judea, in Samaria, and to the ends of the earth."
ACTS 1:7–8 NLT

Let missionaries around the world inspire you, and remember to pray regularly for them, whether you know any personally or not. Missionaries love Jesus and want to share Him with others. Some are doing ministry in countries where it's very dangerous to be a Christian and share the good news of the gospel. They share their faith and hope to lead people to salvation in Jesus Christ, but they do it very carefully because the countries they are in don't give people religious freedom. It takes extraspecial gutsiness and courage to do this kind of missionary work.

Dear God, let missionaries inspire and motivate me. Please bless them as they leave the comforts of their home countries to go where You send them to share Your truth and love. Please protect them from danger. Amen.

Watch Out!

"Watch out for false teachers. They come to you dressed as if they were sheep. On the inside they are hungry wolves. You will know them by their fruit. Do men pick grapes from thorns? Do men pick figs from thistles? It is true, every good tree has good fruit. Every bad tree has bad fruit. A good tree cannot have bad fruit. A bad tree cannot have good fruit. Every tree that does not have good fruit is cut down and thrown into the fire. So you will know them by their fruit."
MATTHEW 7:15–20 NLV

False teachers look harmless like sheep but are dangerous like wolves. We have to be on the lookout and be able to recognize and guard against them. They say they love God and His Word but aren't teaching His Word in honest ways. These people actually try to lead others away from knowing Jesus as their Savior. We will know them by the fruit in their lives, meaning the way they live and the things they do or don't do. We need wisdom from God to be able to spot false teachers and stay away from them and stand against them.

Dear God, please help me to be wise and watchful about false teachers who draw people away from a true saving relationship with You. Amen.

Don't Run from Confrontation

"If another believer sins against you, go privately and point out the offense. If the other person listens and confesses it, you have won that person back. But if you are unsuccessful, take one or two others with you and go back again, so that everything you say may be confirmed by two or three witnesses. If the person still refuses to listen, take your case to the church. Then if he or she won't accept the church's decision, treat that person as a pagan or a corrupt tax collector."
MATTHEW 18:15–17 NLT

Have you ever been scared to face a person who keeps causing you trouble or anxiety? Don't run away in fear. Pray for courage and wisdom about how to confront them. Ask God for good communication when you do confront the person. Let the instructions in His Word lead you. So many times, problems and anxiety in our lives stem from poor communication, but talking things out in a calm and patient way is often a wonderful solution.

Sometimes confronting and communicating don't work out the way we hope. But if you tried your best, you can have peace, knowing that you were gutsy about it with God's help. And you can let God strengthen and teach you through the process.

Dear God, I need courage to confront other people sometimes instead of running away from conflict. Please show me how to do it in wise and effective ways, with good communication and tons of Your grace and love. Amen.

Gideon Was (Eventually) Gutsy

The LORD turned to [Gideon] and said, "Go with the strength you have, and rescue Israel from the Midianites. I am sending you!"

JUDGES 6:14 NLT

He sure wasn't courageous at first (read the whole story in Judges 6), but eventually Gideon was gutsy for God and filled with powerful faith—and the Lord kept speaking to him to show him how to defeat Israel's enemy, the Midianites.

Gideon started with an army of 32,000 men, but then 22,000 gave up. They were too scared to fight. Then God told Gideon He wanted only 300 men to fight against the powerful Midianites, to prove that real power comes from God alone. So with God's power, Gideon and the small army—only 300 men!—rescued Israel from Midian.

At first Gideon was just an ordinary man doing ordinary things. But by trusting God and growing in faith, Gideon went on to do extraordinary, really gutsy things. The same God can empower you to do extraordinary, really gutsy things too.

Dear God, even when I see lots of people giving up all around me, please help me to be brave and remember that You can use anyone and anything, no matter how big or small, to accomplish Your perfect plans. All good victory and power come from You! Amen.

God Created, God Protects

"When you pass through the waters, I will be with you. When you pass through the rivers, they will not flow over you. When you walk through the fire, you will not be burned. The fire will not destroy you. For I am the Lord your God, the Holy One of Israel, Who saves you."
ISAIAH 43:2–3 NLV

If you spend time learning about natural disasters, you could fill yourself with all kinds of fear and maybe lose all your gutsiness! Things like volcanic eruptions, tidal waves, earthquakes, hurricanes, tornadoes, and forest fires are fascinating—but frightening too. No human being can control them or stop them from happening; we can only study them, watch out for them, and make emergency plans for safety during them. Natural disasters should be a reminder to people that no matter how great and smart we humans think we are, we can never control the earth or weather. That's why we should always respect the one true God who can control it all because He created it all. Even if natural disasters make us nervous, we can have peace knowing that our good God loves and protects His children with the promise of eternal life.

Dear God, no matter what happens here on earth, You are the awesome Creator, and I trust in Your love and care! Amen.

The Way to Deal with Enemies

"You have heard that it was said, 'Love your neighbor and hate your enemy.' But I tell you, love your enemies and pray for those who persecute you, that you may be children of your Father in heaven. He causes his sun to rise on the evil and the good, and sends rain on the righteous and the unrighteous."
MATTHEW 5:43–45 NIV

Although it's hard, obeying God's Word about loving our enemies is really gutsy. We can't do it on our own, but we can with God's help. He doesn't mean we have to be bullied or abused. We need to be wise about the ways we show love to enemies. We should always pray for them and ask God to help us love them like He does. We can also do our best to act in kindness and do the right thing even when our enemies don't. We can stand up to them boldly but calmly without being cruel. We can ask God to show us how to love and interact with enemies and stay patient, recognizing that He might work through us to change an enemy's heart.

Dear God, even when it's incredibly hard, please give me the guts and wisdom to love my enemies like You want me to. Show me what to do. I sure can't do it on my own. I love You and want to obey You. Amen.

Pray and Have Peace

Never stop praying.
1 THESSALONIANS 5:17 NLT

You can't be truly gutsy without a lot of prayer. In fact, God's Word tells you never to stop praying. Pause for a moment to think about the fact that the almighty God, the King of Kings and Lord of Lords, wants you to spend time, all the time, talking with Him about anything and everything! It's incredible! Ephesians 6:18 (NLT) says, "Pray in the Spirit at all times and on every occasion. Stay alert and be persistent in your prayers for all believers everywhere." And Philippians 4:6–7 (NLT) says, "Don't worry about anything; instead, pray about everything. Tell God what you need, and thank him for all he has done. Then you will experience God's peace, which exceeds anything we can understand. His peace will guard your hearts and minds as you live in Christ Jesus." Prayer is never pointless; it is powerful—especially as it draws you closer and closer to your perfect, mighty heavenly Father.

Dear God, help me never to forget how important prayer
time with You is. Keep me in conversation with You constantly.
Thank You for wanting to communicate with me. I need
Your help and Your guidance in all things. Amen.

Face Them Head-On

*My Christian brothers, you should be happy when you
have all kinds of tests. You know these prove your faith.
It helps you not to give up. Learn well how to wait so you
will be strong and complete and in need of nothing.*

JAMES 1:2–4 NLV

Your faith is going to be tested in life, and with understanding and the right attitude, you can face those tests head-on. How you respond to the hard things in life proves whether your faith is real—whether you really trust in God or not. When you're going through a test in life, should you throw a fit? Should you quit? Should you get angry at God and give up on faith in Him? Or should you keep trusting that He is in you through His Holy Spirit and will help you and provide for you even if you have to wait awhile for Him to come to the rescue?

**Dear God, help me to face tests with a good attitude. Help me
even to be happy about them because they prove my faith in
You is real if I don't give up in the middle of them. Help me never
to stop trusting You, even when I have to wait on You. Amen.**

He's the God of Hope

May the God of hope fill you with all joy and peace
as you trust in him, so that you may overflow with
hope by the power of the Holy Spirit.
ROMANS 15:13 NIV

Think about the things you hope for in the future, like the kind of family and job you want to have someday. Do you like to journal and pray about those things? Don't ever forget that the reason we have any hope for good things at all is because God is the giver of hope. Every good and perfect gift comes from Him (James 1:17). And our ultimate, final hope is eternity with the Lord in heaven, where there will be no more sickness, sadness, or pain—only perfect paradise forever. As you learn and grow each day, let your hope in God and His good gifts increase more and more—to overflowing!—and become stronger and stronger by the power of the Holy Spirit in you.

Dear God, thank You for giving me hope. I believe every good thing comes from You, and I trust You have good plans for me here on earth and a perfect forever waiting for me in heaven. Amen.

Let Go of Stuff

*"Don't store up treasures here on earth, where moths eat them
and rust destroys them, and where thieves break in and steal.
Store your treasures in heaven, where moths and rust cannot
destroy, and thieves do not break in and steal. Wherever your
treasure is, there the desires of your heart will also be."*
MATTHEW 6:19–21 NLT

We all have favorite items and things that are valuable to us, especially if they
hold special memories. And of course we want to keep some mementoes
of the past! But as we get older and keep accumulating stuff, we realize we
can't hang on to everything forever. Even though it might be sad or overwhelming or just no fun to go through old things and get rid of them, we
have to have the guts to do it. Sharing things we don't have much use for
anymore can be a blessing to others who might be in need. And it creates
space for new things and interests and plans God might have for us. What's
especially important is storing treasure in heaven, and we do that by faithfully
following God and His perfect plans for us.

**Heavenly Father, help me not to hang on too tightly to things
that are just things. Help me to be generous and share, and also
to keep my stuff organized and not overwhelming. Amen.**

Daniel Was Gutsy

Three times a day he got down on his knees and prayed,
giving thanks to his God, just as he had done before.
DANIEL 6:10 NIV

Life had been good for Daniel in the land of Babylon until some jealous leaders went to King Darius and convinced him to make a law that anyone who prayed to someone other than the king would be thrown into the lions' den. But Daniel loved the one true God and continued to pray to Him three times a day in front of his open window. So the jealous leaders reported his actions to the king, and Daniel was thrown into the den of lions.

The next morning, the king hurried to the den and called out, "Has your God been able to save you from the lions?"

And Daniel answered! "My God sent His angel and shut the mouths of the lions. He knows I am not guilty. I have done nothing wrong before you either, O King" (see Daniel 6:20–22).

The king ordered Daniel to be lifted out of the lions' den. Daniel didn't even have a scratch on his body!

Dear God, like Daniel, please help me to be bold and
never stop believing in You and praying to You, even if I'm
in danger for doing so. I trust that You are more powerful
than anything any person can do to me. Amen.

Live Your Best Life

*We are God's masterpiece. He has created us anew in Christ Jesus,
so we can do the good things he planned for us long ago.*
EPHESIANS 2:10 NLT

It's gutsy to choose to trust in Jesus and live for Him. It's a decision that takes a lot of courage every day. To follow Jesus and obey His Word means to do a lot of things differently from what our world and popular culture say is good and cool. You might be ridiculed. You might lose friends. You might be totally misunderstood. You might be left out or rejected or passed up for opportunities. In spite of all that, there is nothing better than knowing and living for the one who created you and has great plans for you! His ways are higher and better than the best things this world has to offer, and He will put you in the places He wants you to be with the people you need in your life. Keep asking Him to show you His plans and His purpose for you, and then do them—because that is truly how to live your best life.

Heavenly Father, I want what You want for me more than anything else. Give me fresh courage and power each day to keep choosing You and Your ways over the ways of this world. I want to follow You and live for You alone! Amen.

Live in God's Shelter

Those who live in the shelter of the Most High will find rest in the shadow of the Almighty. This I declare about the LORD: He alone is my refuge, my place of safety; he is my God, and I trust him. For he will rescue you from every trap and protect you from deadly disease. He will cover you with his feathers. He will shelter you with his wings. His faithful promises are your armor and protection. Do not be afraid of the terrors of the night, nor the arrow that flies in the day. Do not dread the disease that stalks in darkness, nor the disaster that strikes at midday.

PSALM 91:1–6 NLT

God's Word includes powerful promises about the way God takes care of us if we live in His shelter, under His protection. So how do we do that? First, we trust Him as the one true God. We believe in Jesus as our only Savior. We do our best to live according to God's Word. And we stay in close relationship with our heavenly Father. All of those things are awesome anyway, plus we receive the many gifts of God's care on top!

**Dear God, thank You for Your awesome promises
to me in Psalm 91. They make me gutsy!
They give me confidence and courage! Amen.**

No One Could Stop Them

"But before all this happens, men will take hold of you and make it very hard for you. They will give you over to the places of worship and to the prisons. They will bring you in front of kings and the leaders of the people. This will all be done to you because of Me. This will be a time for you to tell about Me. Do not think about what you will say ahead of time. For I will give you wisdom in what to say and I will help you say it. Those who are against you will not be able to stop you or say you are wrong."

LUKE 21:12–15 NLV

Jesus warned His followers that they would find themselves in dangerous trouble because they loved and obeyed Him and preached about Him. Even so, Jesus didn't tell them to give up. He told them to stay strong and not worry, not even about what they would say. He promised to give them wisdom and words and help and power, and He promised that no one would be able to stop them.

Dear Jesus, I never want to give up my faith or stop telling others about You, even if I find myself in trouble or in danger for following You. Help me to stay strong and trust that You will give me wisdom and protection for exactly what I need to do and say. Amen.

Never Tell Lies

Who may climb the mountain of the LORD? Who may stand in his holy place? Only those whose hands and hearts are pure, who do not worship idols and never tell lies. They will receive the LORD's blessing and have a right relationship with God their savior.

PSALM 24:3–5 NLT

The Bible is clear that truth is important, especially in a world where it seems harder and harder to find the truth and where it's popular to make up your own truth. We have to focus on Jesus, whose Word is the ultimate truth (John 14:6), every day of our lives. And we can let scriptures like these remind and warn and inspire us:

- "The honor of good people will lead them, but those who hurt others will be destroyed by their own false ways" (Proverbs 11:3 NLV).

- "A man who tells lies about someone will be punished. He who tells lies will be lost" (Proverbs 19:9 NLV).

- "Teach the words of truth in the right way. Do not listen to foolish talk about things that mean nothing. It only leads people farther away from God" (2 Timothy 2:15–16 NLV).

Dear Jesus, You are truth, and Your Word is ultimate truth. Help me to grow in truth and love and wisdom—and share all these things with others. When I make mistakes and choose dishonesty, please help me to admit my sin. Thank You for Your forgiveness and grace. Amen.

Don't Let Your Courage Melt Away

*The Israelites were paralyzed with fear at this turn
of events, and their courage melted away.*
JOSHUA 7:5 NLT

From this story in Joshua 7, we can learn a good lesson about how our courage or gutsiness can melt away if we're not careful. Take some time to read the whole thing, but the bottom line is that the Israelites had disobeyed God, and He let them be defeated in battle as the consequence of their disobedience. He said, "Israel has sinned and broken my covenant! They have stolen some of the things that I commanded must be set apart for me. And they have not only stolen them but have lied about it and hidden the things among their own belongings. That is why the Israelites are running from their enemies in defeat" (Joshua 7:11–12 NLT). If we disobey and lie and try to hide things from God, He won't fill us with His courage and strength either.

> Dear God, please help me to keep obeying You and Your Word
> and to quickly ask for forgiveness and make things right when
> I make bad choices. I want to keep Your courage and strength
> within me. I don't ever want them to melt away! Amen.

Who Can Be Against You?

If God is for us, who can ever be against us? . . . Who dares
accuse us whom God has chosen for his own? No one—
for God himself has given us right standing with himself.
ROMANS 8:31, 33 NLT

Certain people might cause us worry or fear sometimes, but if we focus on the fact that the Holy Spirit of the one true God Himself is living in us, then truly there is no one powerful enough to ever be against us. No one is greater than our almighty God, who loves us so much that He sent His Son to die to save us. Romans 8:38–39 (NLT) goes on to reassure us, "Nothing can ever separate us from God's love. Neither death nor life, neither angels nor demons, neither our fears for today nor our worries about tomorrow—not even the powers of hell can separate us from God's love. No power in the sky above or in the earth below—indeed, nothing in all creation will ever be able to separate us from the love of God that is revealed in Christ Jesus our Lord."

Almighty God, there is no one else like You, and I'm grateful
to be Your child. Absolutely nothing can keep Your great
love away from me, and that awesome truth fills me
with confidence and courage. Thank You! Amen.

Home Again

"The younger son got together all he had, set off for a distant country and there squandered his wealth in wild living."
LUKE 15:13 NIV

It takes a lot of courage to be willing to admit mistakes and come home again after running away, whether literally or figuratively. So let Jesus' parable about the prodigal son inspire you. One young man took his inheritance from his father and went to a country far away, where he spent everything in wild and foolish living. After all his money was gone, he was hungry, but because of a famine, there was no food in the land he'd run away to. The only job he could find was feeding pigs. Then he began to think about what he'd done and was ashamed. He thought, *I should go home to my father and admit my sins.* So he headed home, and when he was still a long way off, his father saw him and felt compassion. He ran to his son and threw his arms around him. The son said, "Father, I have sinned against heaven and against you. I am not good enough to be called your son." But the father threw a party and said, "Let's be glad, because my son was lost and now he is found."

Heavenly Father, when I've been foolish and run away from Your good ways, help me to be gutsy enough to admit my mistakes and be willing to "come home" to You and to others to make things right. Thank You for Your endless love and grace and mercy. Amen.

God Brings Out the Stars One by One

[God] stretches out the heavens like a canopy, and spreads them out like a tent to live in. . . . "To whom will you compare me? Or who is my equal?" says the Holy One. Lift up your eyes and look to the heavens: Who created all these? He who brings out the starry host one by one and calls forth each of them by name. Because of his great power and mighty strength, not one of them is missing.

ISAIAH 40:22, 25–26 NIV

Look up into the night sky and let it help make you gutsy and brave as you think about this scripture from the book of Isaiah. The one true God who knows you and cares for you made every one of the stars in the sky and calls them all by name. He sits on His throne above all the earth, and there is no one who can ever compare to Him. When the troubles in your life seem great, don't forget who is always greater—God, your heavenly Father, who loves you and lives in you through His Holy Spirit.

Dear God, You are so great that You call out the stars one by one, yet You also love and care about me. That's incredible! Help me be bold and brave and strong as I trust and depend on You. Amen.

When You're Hurting and Confused

*What we suffer now is nothing compared
to the glory he will reveal to us later.*
ROMANS 8:18 NLT

God doesn't always just suddenly fix things the way we hope or expect. We sure wish He would, and we pray and cry to Him, asking Him to see our needs and our fears and to help right away. And if He doesn't, our trust in Him can be shaken. We can be filled with doubt and confusion, maybe even anger and blame toward God. But we have to remember that even when we're hurting and frustrated over prayers that seem to go unanswered, God answers *other* prayers and shows His love and care in many other ways at the same time. We must continue to trust even through awfully sad and scary times. We can't possibly see all the good things God is doing even when life seems hard, but one day in heaven we will understand. Then God will make all things perfect and new. You know what it's like to trust that something works but not know exactly *how* it works, and you can trust God even more!

**Dear God, when I don't see You answering my prayers the
way I hope You will, please let me see how You are providing
in other ways and constantly caring for me. Amen.**

God Is Right and Good in All His Ways

The Lord is right and good in all His ways, and kind in all His works.
The Lord is near to all who call on Him, to all who call on Him in truth.
He will fill the desire of those who fear Him. He will also hear their
cry and will save them. The Lord takes care of all who love Him.
PSALM 145:17–20 NLV

Who is the most trustworthy person you know? Hopefully you're a very trustworthy person too! But no matter how trustworthy and honest anyone on earth is, that person is never perfect in every single thing. Only God is.

Each person we know makes mistakes or lets us down at least once in a while. But as Psalm 145:17 tells us, God is right and good and kind in *all* His ways. He never makes mistakes, and He hears and saves all of us who love and respect Him. Thank God for all the good and trustworthy people in your life, but praise Him most of all for being the one who *never* lets you down! That truth should fill you with endless courage and make you gutsy to face anything that comes your way.

Dear God, I feel confident and fearless when I
remember that You are perfect in all of Your ways
and that You take perfect care of me. Amen.

Being Gutsy While Grieving

Blessed are those who mourn, for they will be comforted.
MATTHEW 5:4 NIV

Moving forward when you've lost a dear family member or friend and are having to figure out how to do life without that person in it takes a whole lot of gutsiness. It's hard to have courage while grieving and missing a close loved one. However, if you know that loved one trusted Jesus as Savior, then you can be confident that he or she is in heaven with God. And with Jesus as your Savior, you can be confident God is with you through the Holy Spirit. There is huge comfort and encouragement in knowing that God is with your loved one and God is with you. So in a way, you are not that far apart at all! It's still sad and hard not to be able to talk with or hug your loved one who has died, of course, but remember that you can always pray like this:

Heavenly Father, I miss my loved one so much. Please give that person a hug for me. Help us to feel close even while we're temporarily apart. Thank You for the confident hope of forever life that You give everyone who trusts in Jesus as Savior. Amen.

God's Unique Plans

The LORD will work out his plans for my life—
for your faithful love, O LORD, endures forever.
PSALM 138:8 NLT

If you've ever watched a squirrel climb higher and higher in a tree, you might marvel at how God made some animals so brave and gutsy, with no fear of heights or of falling. They don't need to be afraid, because God created them to be able to climb high safely. And you probably see other people doing things every day that are just not for you and your personality, and that's okay! God created different things for different purposes, and that includes people designed for different roles and plans and with different kinds of courage and abilities. Each of us only needs to be brave and gutsy for the things God asks of us as we learn from His Word and obey His commandments. He leads each of us uniquely, taking into account the gifts and personalities He has given us.

Dear God, help me to be inspired by the courage I see around me every day—even from squirrels! But also help me to remember that I only need to be gutsy for the unique things You have planned for me to do. I don't need to compare myself with others or be jealous of them. Help me to cheer others on and to cheer myself on too with Your awesome love, power, and encouragement. Amen.

Have the Guts to Help
When No One Else Will

*"Which of these three do you think was a neighbor to the man who fell
into the hands of robbers?" The expert in the law replied, "The one
who had mercy on him." Jesus told him, "Go and do likewise."*
LUKE 10:36–37 NIV

Take some time to read Jesus' parable of the good Samaritan in the Bible.
Jesus shared a story about how violent robbers stole everything from a
Jewish man, even his clothes, and then beat him and left him to die on
the side of the road. Soon a priest came by, saw the poor man, but walked
right past on the other side of the road. Next a man from the family of
Levi passed by, but he didn't help either. Finally a Samaritan man—who
would have normally had *nothing* to do with a Jewish man because Jews
and Samaritans usually hated each other—saw the poor Jewish man lying
by the road. The Samaritan felt sorry for the Jewish man and cared for his
wounds and bandaged them. Then the Samaritan helped the injured man
get to an inn and paid for his stay so he could rest and get well.

Jesus encouraged His followers to be like the Samaritan—to always be
willing to help and care for others, no matter who they are.

**Dear Jesus, please give me the courage I need
to obey You in showing true love and care for
others, no matter who they are. Amen.**

Empowered with Inner Strength

I fall to my knees and pray to the Father, the Creator of everything in heaven and on earth. I pray that from his glorious, unlimited resources he will empower you with inner strength through his Spirit. Then Christ will make his home in your hearts as you trust in him. Your roots will grow down into God's love and keep you strong. And may you have the power to understand, as all God's people should, how wide, how long, how high, and how deep his love is. May you experience the love of Christ, though it is too great to understand fully. Then you will be made complete with all the fullness of life and power that comes from God.
EPHESIANS 3:14–19 NLT

Paul wrote this powerful prayer, and it's for you today too. God's love for you is too big to be measured. And God has unlimited power to strengthen you and make you brave. Jesus lives in you as you trust in Him, and you grow stronger and stronger as you keep your faith in Him. If this awesome truth doesn't make you gutsy, what will?

Dear God, I'm amazed by how much You love me and how You want to empower me. Please keep me learning more about You and growing in faith. Amen.

You Need Backup

Confess your sins to one another and pray for one another.
JAMES 5:16 ESV

To be a gutsy girl who loves and follows Jesus in this world, you need backup. Do you have a strong group of people whom you can talk to about anything and who support you and speak the truth in love to you? Family and friends you can trust with all your concerns? If you are facing a problem or dealing with anxiety, go to them for help and encouragement. Pray with and for one another. Each prayer from your loved ones is a boost to your confidence and courage, coming from God as He hears each prayer and reaches out to help. Galatians 6:2 (NLT) says we should "share each other's burdens, and in this way obey the law of Christ."

Dear God, thank You for family and friends who love me unconditionally and pray for me as we share one another's burdens. Please always bless me with these dear people in my life. Thank You for the way You give me confidence and courage and support through them. Amen.

Speak Boldly About Jesus

There was a lot of grumbling about [Jesus] among the crowds. Some argued, "He's a good man," but others said, "He's nothing but a fraud who deceives the people." But no one had the courage to speak favorably about him in public, for they were afraid of getting in trouble with the Jewish leaders.

<small>JOHN 7:12–13 NLT</small>

When Jesus was teaching on earth, some people who heard Him were interested and thought He was a good man, but they let fear control them and keep them quiet. They didn't want to get in trouble with the Jewish leaders who were saying that Jesus was a liar and a fraud. As you keep maturing, ask God to help you never to be afraid of anyone who says that following Jesus is just a scam or a joke. Those people might seem powerful in this world to ridicule you and try to hurt you, but they are never stronger than God. They can never ruin the good plans He has for you when you stay close to Him and stand strong in your faith. Speak up for Jesus and bravely tell others about Him, how He has saved you, and all the good things He is doing in your life.

Dear Jesus, I am proud of You, and I'm so blessed to know You as my Savior. I want to be gutsy and bold for You and help others to know You too. Amen.

When You Just Can't
Be Friends Anymore

Don't befriend angry people or associate with hot-tempered people,
or you will learn to be like them and endanger your soul.
PROVERBS 22:24–25 NLT

It takes a lot of gutsiness to break away from a bad friendship, but sometimes, sadly, you just have to do it. If a friend you're close to starts making lots of wrong choices or treating others badly, it's not good to stay close friends. You don't want that friend to drag you into sin or trouble. God's Word certainly tells us to share love and kindness and to love our enemies, but it also says, "Bad company corrupts good character" (1 Corinthians 15:33 NLT). We all need wisdom to know how to show love to others without joining them in sin. And sometimes the bravest thing to do is to peacefully but firmly say to someone, "We can't be friends anymore."

Dear God, please give me wisdom about friendships.
Show me if I need to end an unhealthy friendship that's
leading me away from a close relationship with You,
and help me to be gutsy and just do it. Amen.

Ready for Adventure

*May the glory of the LORD continue forever! The LORD takes
pleasure in all he has made! The earth trembles at his glance;
the mountains smoke at his touch. I will sing to the LORD as
long as I live. I will praise my God to my last breath! . . .
Let all that I am praise the LORD. Praise the LORD!*

PSALM 104:31–33, 35 NLT

If you ever go white water rafting or rock climbing or snorkeling in the ocean
or zip-lining high in the trees, you know these types of experiences out in
God's amazing and sometimes dangerous creation can be exhilarating and
fun and scary—all at the same time!

Braving new adventures is good for building your character and helping you be strong and confident. That doesn't mean you have to do crazy
daredevil kinds of things to be gutsy, of course. Just ask God to give you
wisdom and show you the cool experiences that He knows would be good
for you to have throughout your life!

**Dear God, thank You for making the world so full of cool
things to do in Your creation! Guide me and make me
gutsy to try new things according to Your will for my life.
Help me learn and grow through them. Amen.**

Gutsy Like a Lion

*The sinful run away when no one is trying
to catch them, but those who are right with
God have as much strength of heart as a lion.*
PROVERBS 28:1 NLV

This scripture compares people who don't trust Jesus as Savior with people who do. If you are right with God, meaning you have asked Jesus to be your Savior, then you can feel as bold and brave as a lion. That's pretty gutsy! But people who don't trust Jesus as Savior are often so afraid of any little thing that they run even when there is no danger. You can roll your eyes here because that's pretty ridiculous! They might not ever admit their fears, but deep down they have no real faith, nothing truly solid, to give them courage. But all who trust Jesus as Savior have a faith worth believing in. They are right with God because of Jesus and His work on the cross, and so they are able to be as courageous as the mightiest lion.

**Dear Jesus, I trust You, and I know You make me right with
God because You paid the price for my sin on the cross. With
You, I have nothing to fear. My heart is brave and strong
because of You! I am full of power and courage because
of You! You are awesome, and I worship You. Amen.**

Esther Was Gutsy

The king loved Esther more than all the women.
ESTHER 2:17 ESV

Take some time to read the book of Esther in the Bible. King Xerxes of Persia began searching for a new queen, and he liked Esther most of all. She was a Jewish woman, but she'd kept that a secret. Meanwhile, a man named Haman was given a high royal position. Haman wanted all people to bow down and honor him. Esther's cousin Mordecai refused to bow down to anyone but God. Because of this, Haman was filled with hate for Jewish people, and he convinced King Xerxes to order a decree to have them all killed. Mordecai got word to Esther about what was going on. He urged Esther to go to the king and beg for mercy for the Jewish people. But Esther said, "If I go to the king without being invited, I will be killed. The only exception is if the king extends his scepter and spares my life." Mordecai replied, "If you are silent, help will come to the Jews from another place, but you and your father's family will die. So who knows if maybe you became queen to help at exactly a time like this!" (see Esther 4:11, 14).

So Esther went to the king, and he welcomed her. Her life was spared, and because of her faith and courage, God worked through her to save her entire nation.

Dear God, I want to be as faithful and brave as Esther! Amen.

Joy over Fear

Come, let us tell of the LORD's greatness; let us exalt his name together.
I prayed to the LORD, and he answered me. He freed me from all my
fears. Those who look to him for help will be radiant with joy;
no shadow of shame will darken their faces. In my desperation I prayed,
and the LORD listened; he saved me from all my troubles. For the angel
of the LORD is a guard; he surrounds and defends all who fear him.

PSALM 34:3–7 NLT

Name the worries and fears that are in your life right now. Do they go away if you focus on them? How could they? They grow bigger in your mind if you let them have lots of room in there. So don't do that! Instead, give God lots of room in your brain. Look for Him and focus on Him—through reading His Word, singing praises to Him, and praying to Him. Ask Him to show Himself to you in all kinds of ways. Then just wait and see how He pushes away your fears and helps with your worries and makes your face shine with joy!

Dear God, please help me to take my focus off my fears
and to put it on You instead. Fill my mind and heart with
joy because of thoughts of You and praise to You! Amen.

Walk with the Wise, Become Wise

Walk with the wise and become wise, for a companion
of fools suffers harm. Trouble pursues the sinner,
but the righteous are rewarded with good things.
PROVERBS 13:20–21 NIV

Think about the gutsiest people you know. What makes you think they are bold and courageous? Is it their job or career? Is it the hard things they have gone through? Is it how they take care of others? While you're young, it's a great idea to get in the habit of asking thoughtful questions of people older than you who you think are wise and gutsy. Ask them how they got into the job they are in. Or ask what it was like to endure the hard thing they went through. Be willing and happy to have good and deep conversations with adults so that you can learn lessons from those who are older and wiser and more experienced in life and faith than you.

**Dear God, please show me the wise and gutsy people in my
life who I need to learn from. Thank You for their courage,
and help me to build more courage too. Amen.**

It Was by Faith

It was by faith that even Sarah was able to have a child, though she was barren and was too old. She believed that God would keep his promise. And so a whole nation came from this one man who was as good as dead—a nation with so many people that, like the stars in the sky and the sand on the seashore, there is no way to count them. All these people died still believing what God had promised them. They did not receive what was promised, but they saw it all from a distance and welcomed it.
Hebrews 11:11–13 NLT

If you're ever feeling not good enough, not strong enough, not gutsy enough, or simply not enough, go to Hebrews 11 to see examples of Bible heroes who did amazing things, not because of who they were or how good they were or how strong they were or how gutsy they were, but because they had great faith in God. Let their examples help you believe in God's power and might and ability to do absolutely anything in and through you!

Dear God, please grow my faith to be great and then even greater. Through Your Spirit working in me, please use me in powerful ways for Your will and Your glory. Amen.

Habakkuk Had Questions

How long, O LORD, must I call for help? But you do not listen!
"Violence is everywhere!" I cry, but you do not come to save.
HABAKKUK 1:1–2 NLT

Habakkuk had questions, and it's okay if you do too. We can all relate to asking God questions. We sometimes wonder why we have to wait so long on Him or why He doesn't answer our prayers the way we want. Habakkuk was a prophet who spoke for God, and we can learn from him that even though he never got the exact answers he was hoping for from God, he got answers that reminded him of God's power and goodness. Even today in our own lives, we have to keep remembering what Habakkuk learned: that God will work out His perfect plans in His perfect timing.

Dear God, I'm thankful I can ask You questions and know that You always love me and want to help me. Even if I don't get the answers I want, even if I'm confused by You, I still depend on You. I need joy and hope and peace in You. Hold on to me and keep me trusting in Your ways that are so much better than mine. Amen.

Jesus Said You Are the Light

"You are the light of the world. A town built on a hill cannot be hidden. Neither do people light a lamp and put it under a bowl. Instead they put it on its stand, and it gives light to everyone in the house. In the same way, let your light shine before others, that they may see your good deeds and glorify your Father in heaven."
MATTHEW 5:14–16 NIV

Be bold and gutsy as you remember that Jesus said you are the light of the world! With the Holy Spirit in you, your job is to shine your light so that others will want to trust Jesus as Savior and praise God too. We shouldn't ever want to cover up our light. The dark world around us needs the good news and love of Jesus, so let's do good things and be brave to shine as brightly as we can!

Dear Jesus, thank You for calling me the light of the world. The picture conjured by that phrase is so motivating! I want to shine Your love brightly to everyone around me and give God all the praise! Amen.

Jehosheba Was Gutsy

When Athaliah, the mother of King Ahaziah of Judah, learned that her son was dead, she began to destroy the rest of the royal family. But Ahaziah's sister Jehosheba, the daughter of King Jehoram, took Ahaziah's infant son, Joash, and stole him away from among the rest of the king's children, who were about to be killed. She put Joash and his nurse in a bedroom, and they hid him from Athaliah, so the child was not murdered. Joash remained hidden in the Temple of the LORD for six years while Athaliah ruled over the land.

2 KINGS 11:1–3 NLT

Spend some time reading about Jehosheba and her family in 2 Kings 11. She was a princess who proved how gutsy and brave she was when she rescued her young nephew Joash. A queen named Athaliah wanted to kill him, but Jehosheba hid him and his nurse for six years while the evil queen ruled over the land. God used Jehosheba's extraordinary courage to ensure that Joash became the rightful king of Judah.

**Dear God, when I'm needing a good dose of courage,
please help me to remember the gutsiness of Jehosheba.
Please also use me to care for and protect others
and help fulfill Your perfect plans. Amen.**

Refuge and Strength

God is our refuge and strength, always ready to help in times of trouble. So we will not fear when earthquakes come and the mountains crumble into the sea. Let the oceans roar and foam. Let the mountains tremble as the waters surge! A river brings joy to the city of our God, the sacred home of the Most High. God dwells in that city; it cannot be destroyed. From the very break of day, God will protect it. The nations are in chaos, and their kingdoms crumble! God's voice thunders, and the earth melts! The LORD of Heaven's Armies is here among us; the God of Israel is our fortress.

PSALM 46:1–7 NLT

Sometimes we lose our gutsiness and get consumed with worry and fear because we imagine the worst that can happen and then focus on that. So we need this scripture to remind us that there is no horrible thing we can think of that God cannot deal with. He is always our help when we are in trouble, no matter how awful the trouble is. Instead of imagining the worst, we should always think of the best—that God is our refuge and strength in all circumstances!

Dear God, You are my refuge from even the worst kind of trouble. You are my strength. You give me courage. I depend on You! Amen.

Trust Jesus' Promises

"Don't let your hearts be troubled. Trust in God, and trust also in me. There is more than enough room in my Father's home. If this were not so, would I have told you that I am going to prepare a place for you? When everything is ready, I will come and get you, so that you will always be with me where I am. And you know the way to where I am going." "No, we don't know, Lord," Thomas said. "We have no idea where you are going, so how can we know the way?" Jesus told him, "I am the way, the truth, and the life. No one can come to the Father except through me."

JOHN 14:1–6 NLT

The stuff going on in our lives and our homes can be really tough sometimes. But no matter what those circumstances are, we have to keep remembering and trusting Jesus' words and promises. We hold on to great hope in our forever home. And Jesus is our Way, Truth, and Life until we get there.

Dear Jesus, thank You for the perfect home You are making for me in heaven. When life here feels hard, help me to hold on to Your promises. Please lead me and motivate me to press on with joy because You are my Savior! Amen.

God Will Keep You in Perfect Peace

You will keep in perfect peace all who trust in you,
all whose thoughts are fixed on you! Trust in the
LORD always, for the LORD GOD is the eternal Rock.
ISAIAH 26:3–4 NLT

Perfect peace sounds way too good to be true in this world, doesn't it? Something always seems to be ruining our peace, even if it's just family drama or an annoying classmate or a huge school project. But God's Word tells us how to have perfect peace—by trusting in God and fixing our thoughts on Him. When we feel our peace being disrupted, we need to turn our attention back to God and ask for His help to handle what's causing the stress. He wants us to pray about everything! His peace is supernatural and extraordinary. It "exceeds anything we can understand. His peace will guard [our] hearts and minds as [we] live in Christ Jesus" (Philippians 4:7 NLT).

Dear God, I want and need Your perfect peace all the time. When I feel peace slipping from me during stressful situations or even everyday life, please help me to turn my thoughts back to You and keep them there! Amen.

Hannah Was Gutsy

[Hannah] gave him the name Samuel,
saying, "I have asked the Lord for him."
1 SAMUEL 1:20 NLV

Every year Hannah traveled with her husband to a place called Shiloh during a celebration to worship God. And every year she cried and prayed, asking God to bless her with a son. Sometimes she felt as though God had forgotten about her. But still she kept praying. She promised God, "If you give me a son, I will give him back to You for all the days of his life."

A priest named Eli had watched Hannah praying. Then he talked with her and said, "Go peacefully, and may the God of Israel give you what you have asked" (see 1 Samuel 1:11, 17).

Hannah went home with her husband, and soon she did have a son! Hannah loved and cared for Samuel but never forgot her promise to God. When the little boy was old enough, Hannah returned to the tabernacle in Shiloh where she had met Eli. She said, "I asked for my son, and God gave him to me. So now I give him back to God for his whole life" (see 1 Samuel 1:28).

Every year she came back to the tabernacle to visit Samuel. And God blessed her with more children. She was greatly rewarded for being faithful to the Lord. Samuel grew to be an important leader and speaker for God. He was a blessing to all of Israel because Hannah kept her promise.

Dear God, I want to always keep my promises too. Amen

Face Them Fearlessly

Give all your cares to the Lord and He will give you strength.
He will never let those who are right with Him be shaken.
PSALM 55:22 NLV

Have you ever tried to avoid things that make you anxious or afraid? We all can probably think of examples. Take a minute to consider if avoiding or procrastinating really helped, though. Were your fears and anxieties relieved or just delayed? Usually we should confront our fears by asking God for extra courage and facing the task or problem fearlessly in His power. Then we don't have to worry about them hanging around in our minds.

If you find yourself regularly worried or scared, ask God to help you confront those fears rather than avoid them. Facing them will let you see how God's power can work through you to overcome! He loves you and wants to help you with everything! First Peter 5:7 (NIV) says, "Cast all your anxiety on him because he cares for you." *All* of it!

Almighty God, with You working in me, I want to face my fears and worries, not try to avoid them. Please give me courage and help me! Thank You for wanting to take away all my anxiety. Amen.

You'll Never Be Abandoned, Never Be Destroyed

We are pressed on every side by troubles, but we are not crushed.
We are perplexed, but not driven to despair. We are hunted down, but never
abandoned by God. We get knocked down, but we are not destroyed.
2 CORINTHIANS 4:8–9 NLT

We've all had days—maybe even weeks or months or years, unfortunately—when every single thing seems to go wrong. These times can make us feel so discouraged that we wonder when God is *ever* going to step in to help rescue us or at least protect us from any more trouble. But God's Word promises that no matter how discouraged we feel, God will never let us get to a point where we cannot handle the frustration, confusion, pain, and suffering. He will help us endure. We might have to wait awhile, but He will always provide a way out. He lets us experience hard things at times to test and prove our faith, to teach us new lessons, and to show us how brave and strong and gutsy we can be in all kinds of situations when we depend on Him.

Dear God, please help me to keep hanging in there
when I feel discouraged or when I'm suffering. I know
You will never abandon me or let me be destroyed.
You have good plans for me. I trust You always! Amen.

A Mighty Warrior

When the angel of the LORD appeared to Gideon, he said, "The LORD is with you, mighty warrior. . . . Go in the strength you have and save Israel out of Midian's hand. Am I not sending you?" "Pardon me, my lord," Gideon replied, "but how can I save Israel? My clan is the weakest in Manasseh, and I am the least in my family." The LORD answered, "I will be with you."
JUDGES 6:12, 14–16 NIV

Imagine how Gideon must have felt when God spoke to him through an angel's appearance and called him a "mighty warrior." Wow!

Whenever you need a boost of encouragement and bravery, think of God telling you the same thing He told Gideon. You are totally capable of being a mighty warrior for God. He is with you, constantly giving you courage and power. Those qualities don't come from yourself but from God's Holy Spirit within you.

Dear God, I trust that You are with me in everything I do. Do Your will through me by the power of Your Holy Spirit. I want to be a mighty warrior who is gutsy and brave and who points other people to You and Your love and salvation! Amen.

Gutsy While You Have to Wait

Wait for the Lord; be strong, and let your
heart take courage; wait for the Lord!
PSALM 27:14 ESV

Waiting on little things might be annoying, but it's usually no big deal. But what about when you're waiting to hear if someone you love has cancer or not? Or waiting to hear about a job someone desperately needs? Or waiting to hear from loved ones who've been in an accident or are caught in a bad storm? In hard times, waiting can take a whole lot of courage. The time in between the stressful situation and the outcome is often a very scary place to be. Your mind can go a little crazy thinking of all the what-ifs and worries if you let it. So *don't* let it. Focus on scriptures like Psalm 27:14 to calm you. Choose to trust that God is always in control and always works all things together for good for those who love Him (Romans 8:28). He never leaves you, and nothing stops His love for you. Call out to Him in times of waiting, and be patient and brave.

Dear God, please pull me closer to You when I'm waiting and feeling impatient during hard, stressful, and scary times. I don't want worry to take over, and I don't want to make any bad choices during those times. Please give me peace and help me trust You more. Amen.

The Disciples Were Gutsy

*While walking by the Sea of Galilee, he saw two brothers,
Simon (who is called Peter) and Andrew his brother, casting a
net into the sea, for they were fishermen. And he said to them,
"Follow me, and I will make you fishers of men." Immediately they
left their nets and followed him. And going on from there he saw two
other brothers, James the son of Zebedee and John his brother, in the
boat with Zebedee their father, mending their nets, and he called them.
Immediately they left the boat and their father and followed him.*

MATTHEW 4:18–22 ESV

When Jesus started His ministry on earth, He wanted close friends to come alongside Him, travel with Him, learn from Him, and help people believe in Him. He wanted disciples, so He called some men to leave everything that was normal to them and follow Him instead. Think of the courage and faith it must have taken for them to leave the jobs they had known as fishermen to suddenly begin a whole new life with Jesus.

> **Dear Jesus, I want to be gutsy like the disciples.
> If You call to me, I want to be ready to drop
> everything and do anything You ask! Amen.**

Gutsy Because of Good Friends

A friend loves at all times.
PROVERBS 17:17 ESV

Just as Jesus wanted close friends, we need good close friends in our lives too. And it's important to choose wisely. We should want friends who feel as close as family and who encourage us and help us be strong and faithful in carrying out the good plans God has for us. We shouldn't want friends who pull us away from following God or who distract us constantly with meaningless things. We should want real friends who support us through troubles and who help make us sharp! Proverbs 27:17 (NLT) says, "As iron sharpens iron, so a friend sharpens a friend." Of course we want friends to laugh and have fun with, but we should always want those fun times to be God-honoring.

As you think of your current friends, do you have this kind of good friend in your life right now? Is there anyone you need to create distance from? Ask God to help you think wisely about the friendships you have now and the ones you want for the future. He wants to bless you with what is best for you.

Dear God, please bring the right friends into my life according to Your perfect will for me. Amen.

God Will Give the Words

"I am sending you out like sheep among wolves. Therefore be as shrewd as snakes and as innocent as doves. Be on your guard; you will be handed over to the local councils and be flogged in the synagogues. On my account you will be brought before governors and kings as witnesses to them and to the Gentiles. But when they arrest you, do not worry about what to say or how to say it. At that time you will be given what to say, for it will not be you speaking, but the Spirit of your Father speaking through you."

MATTHEW 10:16–20 NIV

Jesus didn't sugarcoat it. He told His disciples that they would go out into dangerous situations where people would hate them because they were His followers. Enemies wouldn't want them to share the good news about Jesus. But Jesus encouraged His friends not to worry about what others would say. The disciples would have exactly the right words because the Spirit of God would speak through them. How cool is that? The Spirit of God can speak through you too.

Dear God, use me as You want to. Speak through me as You want to. Help me to be gutsy and share Your truth and love wherever and whenever You want. I trust that You will give me all the right words. Amen.

New Mornings, New Mercies

Yet I still dare to hope when I remember this: The faithful love of the LORD never ends! His mercies never cease. Great is his faithfulness; his mercies begin afresh each morning. I say to myself, "The LORD is my inheritance; therefore, I will hope in him!" The LORD is good to those who depend on him, to those who search for him.

LAMENTATIONS 3:21–25 NLT

When you wake up to a new day, how do you feel? Hopefully you've gotten some good sleep and you have a fresh start no matter what happened yesterday. God's Word talks about how your heavenly Father's love and mercy are new to you every morning. As you open your eyes and climb out of bed, think of this scripture in Lamentations and let it give you all the gutsiness you need for whatever you're facing in the day ahead.

Heavenly Father, thank You for being so loving and kind and faithful to me! Thank You for brand-new days with fresh starts, days that are filled up again with new supplies of Your grace and mercy. I trust in You and Your power today and every day. Amen.

Remember That You Are Rich

He has made your lives rich in every way. . . . You have the gifts of the Holy Spirit that you need while you wait for the Lord Jesus Christ to come again. Christ will keep you strong until He comes again.

1 CORINTHIANS 1:5, 7–8 NLV

Think of how you have been made "rich in every way." Do you have a gratitude journal where you can list all those ways? If not, can you start one? Listing and focusing on blessings is such a rewarding habit. Being grateful makes you gutsy! When you thank and praise God often for all His goodness to you, it's hard to be worried or afraid or anxious about anything. Ask the Lord to keep showing you specifically how you should use your gifts and blessings in this world until He comes again. Jesus knows you and loves you and will keep you strong until the day of His return!

Dear God, I don't have every material thing in this world, and that's okay, because since I'm Your child, You have truly made me rich in every way that really matters—especially by giving me salvation and eternal life. Thank You for Your power in me. Please keep me strong and help me to use the gifts You have given me in the ways You want me to. Amen.

Let the Proverbs 31 Woman Inspire You

She is more precious than rubies.
PROVERBS 31:10 NLT

The woman described in Proverbs 31 can be a great example to every woman, whether she marries and becomes a wife or not. The Proverbs 31 woman is a hard worker and full of integrity! Let these verses especially inspire you: "She is clothed with strength and dignity, and she laughs without fear of the future. When she speaks, her words are wise, and she gives instructions with kindness. She carefully watches everything in her household and suffers nothing from laziness. Her children stand and bless her. Her husband praises her: 'There are many virtuous and capable women in the world, but you surpass them all!' Charm is deceptive, and beauty does not last; but a woman who fears the LORD will be greatly praised" (Proverbs 31:25–30 NLT).

Dear God, thank You for the example of the woman in Proverbs 31. I want to do my best to live like she did— working hard, loving and inspiring those around me, and most of all, bringing praise to You! Amen.

When You're Mocked and Mistreated

[Jesus said,] "God blesses you when people mock you and persecute you and lie about you and say all sorts of evil things against you because you are my followers. Be happy about it! Be very glad! For a great reward awaits you in heaven. And remember, the ancient prophets were persecuted in the same way."

MATTHEW 5:11–12 NLT

As we faithfully love and follow Jesus in this world, sometimes people will make things harder for us, talk badly about us, and even lie about us. When it happens to you, remember this scripture. Keep being bold and gutsy about your love for Jesus anyway. God sees and knows and cares about it all—and He will reward us in heaven for every hard thing we go through, every mean and mocking thing said against us here on earth. And in heaven, nothing will take away our joy. We'll never have any hard times or hear any ridicule ever again.

Dear Jesus, help me to be bold and gutsy and even happy when I'm being mocked and mistreated because I'm trying to do right and follow You. With Your help, I'll never give up. Amen.

Don't Get Stuck

Fearing people is a dangerous trap,
but trusting the LORD means safety.
PROVERBS 29:25 NLT

Think about a time when you felt trapped, maybe stuck in a difficult situation, your thoughts spinning with endless anxiety. Not knowing how to get out of a bad situation can be super scary and/or stressful.

Proverbs 29:25 says that fearing people is a dangerous trap. We can get our minds stuck in a rut that feels hopeless to get out of if we constantly fear other people. But Hebrews 13:6 (ESV) says, "The Lord is my helper; I will not fear; what can man do to me?" Trusting God as our helper is where our safety is. He is in control of all things and all people, and when we trust Him completely over everything else, He provides us with ultimate safety.

Dear God, I want to fear only You, meaning I respect You.
I don't want to fear any people or situations. When I focus on
You and trust in You completely, I have peace and confidence
that You will keep me safe and come to my rescue. Amen.

Jesus Was Made Just Like Us

It was necessary for [Jesus] to be made in every respect like us, his brothers and sisters, so that he could be our merciful and faithful High Priest before God. Then he could offer a sacrifice that would take away the sins of the people. Since he himself has gone through suffering and testing, he is able to help us when we are being tested.
HEBREWS 2:17–18 NLT

Jesus became a human being just like us. So He knows everything we go through, good times and bad. He "understands our weaknesses, for he faced all of the same testings we do" (Hebrews 4:15 NLT). Thinking about this can help us feel closer to Him and stronger in our faith in Him. We can pray like this:

Dear Jesus, I believe You understand what it's like to be human. You can relate to all my struggles and fears, and knowing that You relate helps me to be strong and brave as I depend on You for help and comfort. I trust that Your Holy Spirit is in me to lead and guide me through every hard thing. I trust that You know, You care, and You love me. Amen.

Don't Drift Away

So we must listen very carefully to the truth we have heard, or we may drift away from it. For the message God delivered through angels has always stood firm, and every violation of the law and every act of disobedience was punished. So what makes us think we can escape if we ignore this great salvation that was first announced by the Lord Jesus himself and then delivered to us by those who heard him speak? And God confirmed the message by giving signs and wonders and various miracles and gifts of the Holy Spirit whenever he chose.
HEBREWS 2:1–4 NLT

You may know people who used to trust in Jesus and the Bible who have now drifted away. Isn't it so sad and discouraging when someone forgets God's truths or just doesn't care about following them anymore? We need to pray for those people and be careful never to let ourselves do the same and drift away from our love of God's Word and our willingness to learn from it. It truly is a lamp for our feet and a light for our path (Psalm 119:105). Without it, we are lost in this world and headed for all kinds of trouble.

> Dear God, I want to follow the truth of Your Word always. Please pull me back quickly and help me listen to You again if I ever start to drift away. Amen.

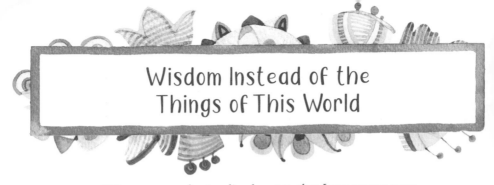

Wisdom Instead of the Things of This World

"Give me an understanding heart so that I can govern your people well and know the difference between right and wrong. For who by himself is able to govern this great people of yours?" The Lord was pleased that Solomon had asked for wisdom.

1 KINGS 3:9–10 NLT

Take some time to read about King Solomon in the Bible—the king who could ask God for anything and chose to ask Him for wisdom. What a good, gutsy guy! Solomon loved God and knew wisdom would be most valuable—because following God's ways of right and wrong and leading others in God's wisdom are things that matter forever, not just for a little while like the things of this world. It takes great courage to be someone who thinks about the things of heaven more than the things of earth (Colossians 3:2).

Let Solomon inspire you. Every time you find yourself faced with a choice to focus either on the things of the world or on God's wise ways of right and wrong, choose God's good ways—which are always the very best!

Dear God, remind me every day of King Solomon. Help me to ask You for wisdom like he did. Help me to use Your perfect wisdom faithfully in all parts of my life. Amen.

Gutsy with God's Wisdom

If any of you lacks wisdom, you should ask God, who gives
generously to all without finding fault, and it will be given to you.
But when you ask, you must believe and not doubt, because the one
who doubts is like a wave of the sea, blown and tossed by the wind.
That person should not expect to receive anything from the Lord.
Such a person is double-minded and unstable in all they do.

JAMES 1:5–8 NIV

When you do ask God for wisdom, don't doubt that He will give it to you. The Bible says God not only gives it but gives it generously. You'll have more than enough. So believe that truth, and then ask God to help you use that wisdom in every single area of your life—at home, with family, at school, at your job, with friends, during sports and activities, when using social media, and on and on. Don't let people who don't love God make you second-guess the wisdom of the Bible and the wisdom God gives through the power of the Holy Spirit working in you.

Dear God, I believe in You and Your Word and that Your ways of right and wrong are wisest and best. Please keep on giving and help me keep on using Your great wisdom. Amen.

With Just a Few Words

And a great windstorm arose, and the waves were breaking into the boat, so that the boat was already filling. But he was in the stern, asleep on the cushion. And they woke him and said to him, "Teacher, do you not care that we are perishing?" And he awoke and rebuked the wind and said to the sea, "Peace! Be still!" And the wind ceased, and there was a great calm. He said to them, "Why are you so afraid? Have you still no faith?" And they were filled with great fear and said to one another, "Who then is this, that even the wind and the sea obey him?"

MARK 4:37–41 ESV

Can you imagine how terrified Jesus' disciples must have been during the storm described in Mark 4? Yet it took only a moment for Jesus to speak and make everything calm again. Remember that the same Jesus who stops storms with just a few words is with you right this moment and every moment of your life. Ask for His help, and let Him lead you constantly.

Dear Jesus, help me to remember this story, and build my faith because of it. You are capable of simply speaking a few words to stop any storm or danger. I believe You are always able to do that in my life too! Amen.

The Lord Is Your Light and Salvation

The Lord is my light and my salvation—so why should I be afraid?
The Lord is my fortress, protecting me from danger, so why should I tremble?
When evil people come to devour me, when my enemies and foes attack
me, they will stumble and fall. Though a mighty army surrounds me,
my heart will not be afraid. Even if I am attacked, I will remain confident.
PSALM 27:1–3 NLT

No matter how old we are, sometimes we still hold on to some fears of the dark. Darkness holds a lot of uncertainty and also possibly hidden dangers, and that's why it can be scary. So be encouraged by this scripture that says God is our light. We don't have to worry about the unknown because He knows it, and He saves us from any hidden dangers. We have nothing to fear with the Lord as our light, our Savior, and our strength.

Dear God, thank You that You are the light, and You are my light. There is no darkness with You, and nothing is hidden from You or unknown by You. You save me and give me strength and courage so that I don't have to fear anyone or anything. Amen.

Mary Was Gutsy

Elizabeth gave a glad cry and exclaimed to Mary, "God has blessed you above all women. . . . You are blessed because you believed that the Lord would do what he said."

LUKE 1:42, 45 NLT

Take some time to read about Mary, the mother of Jesus, in the Bible. In a supernatural way, she was chosen by God to carry and nurture the Savior of the world. And her role sure wouldn't be easy! So her song of praise and her obedience and joy give us an example of what our attitude should be when we are blessed to be chosen by God to do important work for Him, no matter the difficulty. Mary said, "My heart sings with thanks for my Lord. And my spirit is happy in God, the One Who saves from the punishment of sin. The Lord has looked on me, His servant-girl and one who is not important. But from now on all people will honor me. He Who is powerful has done great things for me. His name is holy. The loving-kindness of the Lord is given to the people of all times who honor Him" (Luke 1:46–50 NLV).

Heavenly Father, help me to remember Mary's example of courage and love for You. I want to respond to Your will for my life, no matter how challenging, in the same kind of way she did. Amen.

Be Generous

Remember this—a farmer who plants only a few seeds will get a small crop. But the one who plants generously will get a generous crop. You must each decide in your heart how much to give. And don't give reluctantly or in response to pressure. "For God loves a person who gives cheerfully." And God will generously provide all you need. Then you will always have everything you need and plenty left over to share with others.
2 CORINTHIANS 9:6–8 NLT

Being generous is gutsy. You have to be brave to give away what you have to others because you have to trust that you will still have what you need. No worries! God will always give you enough for your own needs as you help provide for the needs of others. The Bible promises it. The more you give, the more God will give you. He loves to reward you when you share the gifts that ultimately always come from Him.

Dear God, I want to give to others cheerfully and bravely without any worries. I don't ever want to be afraid of not having enough for myself. I trust that You will always provide for and bless me. Amen.

Heads Up!

"And now, compelled by the Spirit, I am going to Jerusalem, not knowing what will happen to me there. I only know that in every city the Holy Spirit warns me that prison and hardships are facing me. However, I consider my life worth nothing to me; my only aim is to finish the race and complete the task the Lord Jesus has given me—the task of testifying to the good news of God's grace."

ACTS 20:22–24 NIV

The Holy Spirit gave Paul a heads-up that he would face hardship—like time in prison, for example. But Paul still felt led to go to Jerusalem. He knew he was supposed to do the work of telling others the good news about Jesus saving people from their sins. Paul said his life was worth nothing unless he did this work. Paul can inspire us today to know that even when the Holy Spirit gives us a heads-up that hard times are coming, we can still be gutsy and faithful to do the good works that God asks us to do—especially sharing His love and the truth about Jesus.

Dear God, through Your Holy Spirit, please warn me when trouble is coming, but don't let me be afraid of it or let it stop me from doing what You ask me to do in the midst of it. Amen.

The Powerful One Who Wins the Battle

*Have joy and be happy with all your heart, O people of Jerusalem!
The Lord has taken away your punishment. He has taken away
those who hate you. The King of Israel, the Lord, is with you. You
will not be afraid of trouble any more. On that day it will be said to
Jerusalem: "Do not be afraid, O Zion. Do not let your hands lose
their strength. The Lord your God is with you, a Powerful One Who
wins the battle. He will have much joy over you. With His love He will
give you new life. He will have joy over you with loud singing."*
ZEPHANIAH 3:14–17 NLV

The words of the prophet Zephaniah can encourage you today just as they encouraged the people of Jerusalem in ancient times. No matter what problem or pain you're going through, no matter what enemy is working against you, the almighty God wins every battle for you in the end because He's giving you eternal life. Keep on trusting Him and asking Him to make you gutsy and brave.

**Dear God, I trust that You ultimately win every battle.
There is no one mightier than You. Thank You for Your joy
and victory in my life, both now and forever. Amen.**

Agabus Stood Up and Spoke

At that time some men who preached God's Word came to Antioch and told what was going to happen. They were from Jerusalem. One of them was Agabus. The Holy Spirit told him to stand up and speak. He told them there would be very little food to eat over all the world. This happened when Claudius was leader of the country. The Christians agreed that each one should give what money he could to help the Christians living in Judea. They did this and sent it to the church leaders with Barnabas and Saul.

ACTS 11:27–30 NLV

When the Holy Spirit told Agabus to stand up and speak, he did it. And because Agabus was obedient, he was able to help take care of other Christians who might soon have been starving. When we obey the Holy Spirit, God helps us, and He helps others through us too. We should always be listening for the Lord's voice and be ready and willing to do anything He asks through His Holy Spirit within us.

> Dear God, I want to stand up and speak anytime You ask me to, just like Agabus did. Help me to listen well for You and to be gutsy to obey You without hesitation. Amen.

You Are Free from the Power of Sin and Death

Now, because of this, those who belong to Christ will not suffer the punishment of sin. The power of the Holy Spirit has made me free from the power of sin and death. This power is mine because I belong to Christ Jesus.

ROMANS 8:1–2 NLV

With Jesus as your Savior, you are totally free from the power of sin and death. Let those words sink in and strengthen your courage and hope. Yes, we are sadly all affected by sin and death in many different, awful ways. But with Jesus as our Savior, we are never enslaved to sin or defeated by sin. These words from Paul in the book of Romans are words you can make your own. If you belong to Jesus because you have asked Him to be your Savior, you will not suffer the punishment of sin. Of course our earthly bodies will have hard times in this world, and someday we will die, but our souls will never die. We will gain new bodies and go on to eternal life with Jesus— a perfect, pain- and trouble-free forever on the new earth.

Dear God, thank You for making me free from the power of sin and death. The power of the Holy Spirit is mine because I believe in and am saved by the work of Your Son, Jesus, on the cross to pay for my sin! I'm so grateful! Amen.

So Gutsy, She Gave It All

*Many rich people put in large sums. And a poor
widow came and put in two small copper coins.*
MARK 12:41–42 ESV

One day Jesus watched as many rich people gave large offerings to God at the temple. This wasn't hard for them to do because they were so rich that they had plenty of money to share. But then Jesus watched a poor widow drop in two very small copper coins. The two coins weren't even worth a total of one cent.

Jesus said to His disciples, "This poor widow has given more money than all the others."

What? The widow had only given two small coins that didn't even amount to a penny!

But Jesus said, "The rich people put in money they didn't even need because they have so much extra. But the poor widow has nothing extra. She needed every bit of her money to live on, but still she gave it all to God" (see Mark 12:43–44).

**Dear God, help me to be gutsy about giving, like the widow
was in this passage from Mark. She trusted You to provide for
her no matter what, even if she gave until she had nothing left.
I want to give to You in that same fearless kind of way. Amen.**

Crank Up the Music!

Call out with joy to the Lord, all the earth. Be glad as you serve the Lord. Come before Him with songs of joy. Know that the Lord is God. It is He Who made us, and not we ourselves. We are His people and the sheep of His field. Go into His gates giving thanks and into His holy place with praise. Give thanks to Him. Honor His name. For the Lord is good. His loving-kindness lasts forever. And He is faithful to all people and to all their children-to-come.

PSALM 100 NLV

Sometimes we just need to crank up some good music when we need more courage and gutsiness to face our problems and stress. Especially worship songs! Praising God and singing about Him reminds us of His power and goodness. He is the very best source of confidence and courage for any new thing we're about to do or any hard situation we are in.

Dear God, please help me to have joy and be able to sing even when I'm feeling anxious or afraid. I know music can help calm me down and strengthen me—especially songs of praise to You! Amen.

You're a Masterpiece. . .Don't Forget It

For we are God's masterpiece. He has created us anew in Christ Jesus, so we can do the good things he planned for us long ago.
EPHESIANS 2:10 NLT

God created this amazing world and everything in it, but His very best work includes you! Other versions of the Bible use the words *handiwork* and *workmanship* in this verse, but think about the word *masterpiece* for a minute. What an inspiring honor to be described that way! Nothing else in all creation is as wonderful and valuable as people because nothing else in all creation is created in God's image. And when God creates people, He has special plans for each one of us to do good things. You're so much more than just a gutsy girl—you are a *masterpiece*, and your Master is in you through His Spirit, helping you to accomplish all the amazing things He designed you for.

Dear God, thank You for being my good Master and for making me a masterpiece. I feel treasured and cherished and so dearly loved when I think about how You value me, how You created me and designed the plans for my life. Show me those good plans and lead me in them every day. Amen.

Angels Have Your Back

"Daniel, servant of the living God, has your God, Whom you always serve, been able to save you from the lions?" Then Daniel said to the king, "O king, live forever! My God sent His angel and shut the lions' mouths. They have not hurt me."

DANIEL 6:20–22 NLV

God could have saved Daniel in any way He chose—such as enabling Daniel to fly out of the den, killing the lions instantly, or making the king switch places with Daniel. But God sent His angel to shut the mouths of the lions. Angels are real, and it's important to learn about them—not from what movies and stories say but from what God's Word says. God can send His angels to help you at any moment for any reason in ways you might never even realize. Hebrews 1:14 (NLV) says, "Are not all the angels spirits who work for God? They are sent out to help those who are to be saved from the punishment of sin."

Dear God, thank You that angels are real. Teach me about them according to Your Word. Please send them to me when I need them. Thank You for Your mighty love, protection, and care! Amen.

Reject False Teaching;
Hold Tight to the Truth

*All of us are to be as one in the faith and in knowing the Son of God.
We are to be full-grown Christians standing as high and complete as Christ
is Himself. Then we will not be as children any longer. Children are like
boats thrown up and down on big waves. They are blown with the wind.
False teaching is like the wind. False teachers try everything possible to make
people believe a lie, but we are to hold to the truth with love in our hearts.*
EPHESIANS 4:13–15 NLV

Every day it seems there are more confusing things in the world, more people telling us that it's not loving or kind to tell the truth about Jesus and the truth found in God's Word. We constantly have to ask the Holy Spirit within us to give us the wisdom to know what is false teaching and what is not. We must ask Him to help us keep maturing in our faith while holding tightly to God's truth and growing in our desire to share Him with others.

Dear God, please help me never to be blown around by false teaching. Keep me attached tightly to Your truth. Keep Your love in my heart as I share Your truth with others. Amen.

Keep Safe in God's Love

*But you, dear friends, must build each other up in your most
holy faith, pray in the power of the Holy Spirit, and await the
mercy of our Lord Jesus Christ, who will bring you eternal life.
In this way, you will keep yourselves safe in God's love.*
JUDE 1:20–21 NLT

Are you keeping yourself safe in God's love, like this scripture says? Do you spend time learning from God? Do you regularly read His Word? Do you talk to God through prayer and have quiet time to listen for answers? Do you attend a good Bible-teaching church to worship and learn and serve there? Do you have strong Christians in your life who help encourage you and remind you of God's truth and love? Do you fill your mind with songs of praise to Him? These are all awesome ways to keep yourself safe in the love of God! Because His Holy Spirit lives within you, He never leaves you, but sometimes it's easy to ignore that He is there. So remember to keep yourself safe in His love every moment of every day.

**Dear God, I want to keep myself safe in Your love,
staying in close relationship with You! Please help
me never to forget or ignore You. Amen.**

Just Embrace the Weirdness

Dear friends, your real home is not here on earth. You are strangers here. I ask you to keep away from all the sinful desires of the flesh. These things fight to get hold of your soul.

1 PETER 2:11 NLV

Maybe sometimes you feel like a weirdo, trying to be cool in this world but somehow never quite getting there. Guess what? You *should* be a weirdo if you are following close to Jesus! Just embrace the weirdness and be gutsy about it. It's a good thing, the best kind of weird. The Bible talks about how we are strangers here on earth because our real home is in heaven. You have been set apart by God as His child because of your faith in Jesus, and you have the Holy Spirit within you. That doesn't mean you should try to be a weirdo who is obnoxious or annoying or unloving. It just means you often won't fit in with what's popular in the world, because so often what is popular in the world is disobedience to God.

Dear God, please help me to be at peace with feeling like a stranger and weirdo here on earth. Remind me that my purpose is not to fit in with what's cool and popular. My purpose is to follow You, doing the good things You have planned for me and sharing Your truth and love with others as You lead me. Amen.

Peter Was Gutsy

*Peter answered him, "Lord, if it is you,
command me to come to you on the water."*
MATTHEW 14:28 ESV

One time when Jesus went off to pray alone, the disciples were in a boat traveling on ahead of Him. Then, in the middle of the night, He walked out on the lake to catch up with them. The Bible says the disciples were terrified, thinking Jesus was a ghost. But Jesus immediately said to them, "It is I. Do not be afraid" (Matthew 14:27 ESV).

As soon as the disciple Peter heard it was Jesus out on the lake, he wanted to walk on water too, and he trusted that Jesus could make that happen. So he climbed out of the boat and started out just fine walking on the waves toward Jesus. But then something changed. He noticed the weather and began to sink. Peter took his focus off Jesus and put it on his fear of the wind and waves instead. The same thing will happen to us if we let it. We have to keep our focus on Jesus through all the ups and downs, fears and anxieties of life. If we do, He'll keep us brave and steady; but if we don't, we will begin to sink.

Dear Jesus, I don't want to lose focus on You and Your power to do anything! Please help me never to sink away from You! Amen.

Feed Yourself Well

Then Jesus was led by the Spirit into the wilderness to be tempted by the devil. After fasting forty days and forty nights, he was hungry. The tempter came to him and said, "If you are the Son of God, tell these stones to become bread." Jesus answered, "It is written: 'Man shall not live on bread alone, but on every word that comes from the mouth of God.'"

MATTHEW 4:1–4 NIV

If you don't eat all day, what happens? You feel awful, right? Your stomach growls and hurts, and maybe your head hurts too. You feel tired and weak. We all need food, and we can't last too long without it. But even more important than food for our physical health, we need food for our spiritual and mental health. We find that kind of food in the truth of God's words. So just like we usually feed our bodies with breakfast, lunch, and dinner (and probably some good snacks in between!), we need to feed our hearts and minds and souls with God's good truth in the Bible to strengthen and nourish and encourage us.

Dear God, remind me that I can't be gutsy unless I'm spiritually and mentally and emotionally healthy by feeding on Your Word! Amen.

Put On God's Armor

Put on every piece of God's armor so you will be able to resist the enemy in the time of evil. Then after the battle you will still be standing firm. Stand your ground, putting on the belt of truth and the body armor of God's righteousness. For shoes, put on the peace that comes from the Good News so that you will be fully prepared. In addition to all of these, hold up the shield of faith to stop the fiery arrows of the devil. Put on salvation as your helmet, and take the sword of the Spirit, which is the word of God.
EPHESIANS 6:13–17 NLT

You probably know what it's like to put on some clothes you look nice in and instantly feel more confident. A favorite outfit that you know looks good feels good too! An athlete feels more confident and ready to play with a uniform and the appropriate gear. And a soldier going into battle absolutely needs protective armor. God tells us that as Christians, we need our strong suit on as well—a special kind of spiritual armor to wear as we fight the spiritual battles going on around us at all times.

Dear God, thank You for wanting to protect and equip us with exactly what we need to be strong, gutsy, and able to fight against evil. Amen.

God Will Never Fail or Forsake You

David also said to Solomon his son, "Be strong and courageous, and do the work. Do not be afraid or discouraged, for the LORD God, my God, is with you. He will not fail you or forsake you."
1 CHRONICLES 28:20 NIV

All kinds of situations require you to have courage and be gutsy. Some situations might seem silly and small in the grand scheme of things, and others are a really big deal. But big or small, God cares deeply about every situation you're in. He wants you to depend on Him and His power and remember that whatever is going on in your life, He won't ever fail or forsake you. The passage of scripture from 1 Chronicles in the Bible is a pep talk from King David to his son Solomon, but the words are for you today as well—to encourage and inspire and strengthen you.

Dear God, You are the giver of all courage. Help me to be strong and gutsy because of Your Spirit living in me, loving me, encouraging me, and empowering me. Remind me of the good pep talks in Your Word that motivate and strengthen me even today. Amen.

Deborah Was Gutsy

Deborah, a woman who spoke for God, was judging Israel at that time. . . . And the people of Israel came to her to find out what was right or wrong. She sent for Barak. . .and said to him, "The Lord, the God of Israel, says, 'Go to Mount Tabor. . . .' " Then Barak said to her, "I will go if you go with me. But if you do not go with me, I will not go." And she said, "For sure I will go with you. But the honor will not be yours as you go on your way. For the Lord will sell Sisera into the hands of a woman."
JUDGES 4:4–6, 8–9 NLV

Deborah was the only female judge of the people of Israel. Back in Bible times, when most women were considered far less valuable than men, the fact that she was in such a high position was a really big deal. God surely was helping her to be gutsy and brave. She was a "woman who spoke for God." Let Deborah inspire you to be a woman who speaks for God too. Let Him help you know right from wrong, and let Him lead you and speak through you to others who need to hear His truth and love.

Dear God, help me to be gutsy like Deborah, speaking for You and knowing Your ways of right and wrong. Amen.

Don't Be Afraid of Anyone

[Jesus said,] "But don't be afraid of those who threaten you. For the time is coming when everything that is covered will be revealed, and all that is secret will be made known to all. . . . Don't be afraid of those who want to kill your body; they cannot touch your soul. Fear only God, who can destroy both soul and body in hell. What is the price of two sparrows—one copper coin? But not a single sparrow can fall to the ground without your Father knowing it. And the very hairs on your head are all numbered. So don't be afraid; you are more valuable to God than a whole flock of sparrows."
MATTHEW 10:26, 28–31 NLT

If you've ever dealt with enemies or people doing evil, you know they usually try to stay in darkness (both literally and figuratively) and keep things hidden. This scripture reminds you not to be afraid of them, for their evil deeds will be brought into the light and revealed—if not right away, then eventually. Ultimately God sees and cares and will bring consequences and justice. Keep asking Him to do that, and pray for wisdom regarding how to stand against evil and enemies—and for protection and courage too!

Dear God, remind me all the time that I don't need to be afraid of anyone. You see and know every evil, and You will bring justice and punishment and make everything right in Your perfect timing. Amen.

Learn from Peter's Denial

The guards lit a fire in the middle of the courtyard and sat around it,
and Peter joined them there. A servant girl noticed him in the firelight
and began staring at him. Finally she said, "This man was one of Jesus'
followers!" But Peter denied it. "Woman," he said, "I don't even know him!"
LUKE 22:55–57 NLT

The same Peter who was gutsy enough to step out and walk toward Jesus on water was also the one who later denied even knowing Jesus. Three times, actually! When Jesus had been arrested and was about to be crucified, Peter felt too afraid of what the people might do to him if he showed loyalty to Jesus. And then Peter felt ashamed for denying his Lord. He cried bitterly. Even after Peter made such a sad mistake, Jesus loved and forgave him, and Peter went on to do great things to spread the news of Jesus.

Dear Jesus, I don't ever want to deny You like Peter did. I sure hope
I never do. But in whatever ways I might make mistakes, please
help me remember how Peter messed up yet You loved and forgave
him when he was sorry. You are full of grace and mercy, and I
will continue to live for You and share Your good news. Amen.

Birds Help Make You Brave

"Not one of the birds falls to the earth without your Father knowing it. God knows how many hairs you have on your head. So do not be afraid. You are more important than many small birds."
MATTHEW 10:29–31 NLV

Every time you see a bird fly or hear its song, think of this scripture and let it fill you up with courage as it reminds you that God knows every single bird that lives on the earth at every moment. He knows exactly where it is and what it does. And He also knows you so well that He has even counted the hairs on your head. No one else knows and loves you that much! God cares about you and protects you. You are so important to Him that He literally let His Son die to take away your sin and save you. Don't ever forget that truth, gutsy girl, and let every bird help make you feel bold and brave and cherished by God.

Dear God, I can't even begin to understand how You know everything about everything—plus everything about me too. But I am grateful for Your love and care. I'm especially grateful that You gave Jesus to save me from my sin. Amen.

A Gutsy Young King

Josiah was eight years old when he became king. He ruled for thirty-one years in Jerusalem. His mother's name was Jedidah the daughter of Adaiah of Bozkath. Josiah did what is right in the eyes of the Lord. He walked in all the way of his father David. He did not turn aside to the right or to the left.

2 KINGS 22:1–2 NLV

King Josiah became king at only eight years old, and it's hard to imagine someone so young yet so gutsy! What would you do in his shoes? Hopefully you'd want to be a lot like he was, because the Bible says he "did what is right in the eyes of the Lord." That should also be our goal in everything we do, even if we never become royal rulers. We are, in fact, always leaders to others as long as we are following Jesus—because people who don't yet follow Jesus look to us to lead them to His love and truth.

Dear God, I want to be like Josiah, doing what is right in Your eyes. I want to be gutsy and focus on following You. Please help me so that I can do Your will and lead others to You! Amen.

Be Ready for the Lord's Best Work

In a wealthy home some utensils are made of gold and silver, and some are made of wood and clay. The expensive utensils are used for special occasions, and the cheap ones are for everyday use. If you keep yourself pure, you will be a special utensil for honorable use. Your life will be clean, and you will be ready for the Master to use you for every good work. Run from anything that stimulates youthful lusts. Instead, pursue righteous living, faithfulness, love, and peace. Enjoy the companionship of those who call on the Lord with pure hearts.

2 TIMOTHY 2:20–22 NLT

It takes a lot of gutsiness to stay pure and run away from sin in this messed-up world. But this scripture encourages you to do so. Think about how you want God to use your life. Do you want to be just like regular everyday wood and clay, or do you want to be like shining gold used for better purposes? When you work hard to live a clean life, staying as far away from sin as possible, God can use you for the very best things He has planned.

Lord, please keep showing me which areas of my life need to be purified. Help me to stay far away from the sinful things that are bad for me. Use my life in the wonderful ways You created me for. Amen.

God Won't Leave You

"You are a forgiving God. You are kind and loving, slow to anger, and full of loving-kindness. You did not leave them. They even melted gold and made a calf, and said, 'This is your God Who brought you up from Egypt.' They spoke sinful words against You. But You, in Your great loving-kindness, did not leave them in the desert. The pillar of cloud which led them on their way during the day did not leave them. And the pillar of fire which gave light to the way they were to go during the night did not leave them. You gave Your good Spirit to teach them. You did not keep Your bread from heaven from their mouths. And You gave them water when they were thirsty. For forty years You kept them alive in the desert and gave them everything they needed."

NEHEMIAH 9:17–21 NLV

Our heavenly Father is patient even when His people treat Him badly. He never leaves. He is forgiving and loving. He provides for His people and teaches us through His Holy Spirit. This scripture might be about ancient times and ancient people, but you can apply the truth in it to your own life today.

Dear God, thank You for loving Your people, including me, so well. Please forgive me when I treat You badly and sin against You. Thank You for being full of mercy and grace. Amen.

Fill Your Mind and Heart with Praise

Praise the Lord! Praise God in his sanctuary; praise him in his mighty heavens! Praise him for his mighty deeds; praise him according to his excellent greatness! Praise him with trumpet sound; praise him with lute and harp! Praise him with tambourine and dance; praise him with strings and pipe! Praise him with sounding cymbals; praise him with loud clashing cymbals! Let everything that has breath praise the Lord! Praise the Lord!

PSALM 150 ESV

Did you catch the theme in this scripture? What are we supposed to do? *Praise the Lord*—everywhere for everything in all kinds of ways! We can be gutsy plus so much more when we are full of praise to God, because constantly praising God means we are constantly aware of His greatness and power. When we focus on that greatness and power as well as His never-ending love and care for us, we have absolutely nothing to fear.

Dear God, yes, I praise You! You are awesome! You are greater and mightier than any problem or enemy I will ever face. I have nothing to fear when I'm praising and trusting You! Amen.

Let Lydia Inspire You

On the Sabbath we went outside the city gate to the river, where we expected to find a place of prayer. We sat down and began to speak to the women who had gathered there. One of those listening was a woman from the city of Thyatira named Lydia, a dealer in purple cloth. She was a worshiper of God. The Lord opened her heart to respond to Paul's message.

ACTS 16:13–14 NIV

A woman named Lydia in the Bible had a business selling purple cloth, and because purple was the color of royalty, she probably made a lot of money. Sometimes people with a lot of money think they don't need anything else in their lives except money. You probably know people like that. They think they can buy any kind of happiness and peace. But Lydia worshipped God and wanted to listen to what the followers of Jesus had to say. And the Bible says the Lord "opened her heart" and she accepted Jesus as her Savior. He alone gives true happiness, peace, and everlasting life!

Dear God, no matter what good things or how much money I am blessed with in this life, I still need You and salvation through Jesus. Thank You for Lydia's example to me. Help me to share her example with others. Amen.

Put the Lord in Front

I will give honor and thanks to the Lord, Who has told me what to do. Yes, even at night my mind teaches me. I have placed the Lord always in front of me. Because He is at my right hand, I will not be moved. And so my heart is glad. My soul is full of joy. My body also will rest without fear. For You will not give me over to the grave. And You will not allow Your Holy One to return to dust.

PSALM 16:7–10 NLV

Are you always putting the Lord in front of you? It's the best way to live! Let God lead, because when you do, you will be steady and stable in every area of your life—even when hard and sad and painful times hit. No matter what comes your way, God will give you joy and peace and rest without fear.

Dear God, please help me not to want to be the leader of my life. I want to honestly be able to say that I always put You in front of me. I know You will lead me far better than I can lead, for You are perfect and worthy of all praise! Amen.

When It's God's Fight, Not Yours

He said, "Listen, all you people of Judah and Jerusalem! Listen, King Jehoshaphat! This is what the LORD says: Do not be afraid! Don't be discouraged by this mighty army, for the battle is not yours, but God's. Tomorrow, march out against them. . . . But you will not even need to fight. Take your positions; then stand still and watch the LORD's victory. He is with you, O people of Judah and Jerusalem. Do not be afraid or discouraged. Go out against them tomorrow, for the LORD is with you!"

2 CHRONICLES 20:15–17 NLT

When a problem in your life seems way too overwhelming, remember this Bible story. God told His people, who were up against a great enemy army, that the battle was not theirs but His. He told them they wouldn't even need to fight. They could just stand and watch His saving power do all the hard work for them. Sometimes all you need to do to be gutsy is stand strong in your faith and watch the miracles God does to rescue you from trouble.

Dear God, show me when I just need to stand still and strong in faith and let You do all the fighting for me. Thank You, thank You, thank You! Amen.

Zacchaeus Was Gutsy

[Zacchaeus] was seeking to see who Jesus was.
LUKE 19:3 ESV

Zacchaeus was a wealthy man, a chief tax collector who lived in Jesus' time. Men like him were known for cheating and taking too much of other people's money. So most people in Jericho hated and avoided him.

But Zacchaeus was drawn to Jesus and wanted to do whatever it took to see Him as He traveled through Jericho. Zacchaeus was short, so he ran ahead of where Jesus would walk and climbed a big tree. With a good view from high in the branches, he waited and watched for Jesus.

When Jesus passed by, He stopped and spotted Zacchaeus. He called him by name and said, "Come down right away. I am going to your house today."

Zacchaeus was thrilled as he climbed down and welcomed Jesus to his home.

As Zacchaeus spent time with Jesus, he was sorry for his sins and wanted to make all his wrongs right. He wanted to help the poor and give back to people all the money he had cheated them out of—plus four times more.

Dear God, I want to be gutsy like Zacchaeus, who was so eager to see You and welcome You—and so brave to admit his mistakes and then do all he could to correct them. Amen.

Almighty God Is Holding You Up

*"So do not fear, for I am with you; do not be dismayed, for I am your God. I will strengthen you and help you; I will uphold you with my righteous right hand. All who rage against you will surely be ashamed and disgraced; those who oppose you will be as nothing and perish. Though you search for your enemies, you will not find them. Those who wage war against you will be as nothing at all. For I am the L*ORD *your God who takes hold of your right hand and says to you, Do not fear; I will help you."*
ISAIAH 41:10–13 NIV

God gave these words through His prophet Isaiah to the people of Israel. But these words are also for you to remember today so that they will give you strength and courage and make you gutsy! Is anyone mad at you or fighting against you? Don't sweat it! Look to almighty God for help, guidance, and protection. You'll be okay because He is with you, always holding your hand, always holding you up, always helping you.

Heavenly Father, I don't want to be afraid of anyone or anything. You are the one true almighty God who helps me and holds me up. Please don't ever let me forget that. Amen.

Be Gutsy with the Good News

I am not ashamed of the Good News. It is the power of God. It is the way He saves men from the punishment of their sins if they put their trust in Him. It is for the Jew first and for all other people also. The Good News tells us we are made right with God by faith in Him. Then, by faith we live that new life through Him.

ROMANS 1:16–17 NLV

Everyone loves and needs good news, right? The best good news is God's good news—that He sent His perfect Son, Jesus, to earth to live among us and show His love and power and then die for us as payment for our sin. Then He rose again to show He conquered sin and death and that God gives eternal life to all who believe in Him. We're never supposed to keep this powerful good news to ourselves. We have to be gutsy and spread it around to everyone we can!

Dear God, remind me that Your good news has the power to save people from sin. I don't ever want to be ashamed of it. Make me bold and gutsy to share it everywhere! Amen.

They Wouldn't Stop Worshipping

About midnight Paul and Silas were praying and singing hymns to God, and the prisoners were listening to them.
ACTS 16:25 ESV

On one of Paul's many travels, he and his friend Silas were put in jail. But they kept a strong and gutsy faith anyway. In fact, they used their jail time to pray and sing to God. Late at night while they were worshipping and other prisoners were listening to them, suddenly an earthquake shook the jail and the prison doors flew open and everyone's chains broke loose! The jailer woke up and was terrified. He thought he would be killed as punishment for all the prisoners going free. But Paul said to him, "We are all here!" The jailer ran to Paul and Silas and dropped to the ground in front of them. Then he brought them out of their jail cell and said, "What must I do to be saved?"

They told him, "Believe in the Lord Jesus, and you will be saved, you and your household" (Acts 16:30–31 ESV).

Then the jailer took Paul and Silas to his home and fed them a meal. Everyone in his family listened to Paul and Silas and believed in Jesus.

Dear God, I won't stop worshipping You either, no matter my circumstances! You are the God of awesome miracles and merciful salvation, and I praise You! Amen.

Be Gutsy on God's Path, Not Your Own

Trust in the LORD with all your heart and lean not on your own understanding;
in all your ways submit to him, and he will make your paths straight.
PROVERBS 3:5–6 NIV

You might hear the advice "Follow your heart" a lot these days, often from nice people with good intentions. But that's not always great advice. Before any of us really do follow our own hearts, we need to make sure our hearts match up with God's. Our own hearts and desires are frequently tempted by sin and everything that's bad for us. So God's Word tells us to trust Him with all our hearts and *not* to lean on our own understanding. We need to stay close to Him by reading His Word, praying, worshipping Him, and serving Him, as well as by fellowshipping with and learning from other strong believers. And we constantly need to ask God to help us submit to Him and His will for us—that's the only way we stay on His good, straight paths.

Lord, I want to trust in You and Your path more than in myself.
Please help me to follow my heart only when it's in tune with
Yours because I'm submitted to You and Your will. Amen.

You Are Royalty!

All who are led by the Spirit of God are children of God. So you have not received a spirit that makes you fearful slaves. Instead, you received God's Spirit when he adopted you as his own children. Now we call him, "Abba, Father." For his Spirit joins with our spirit to affirm that we are God's children. And since we are his children, we are his heirs.

<small>ROMANS 8:14–17 NLT</small>

You are true royalty as a daughter of the one true King, and you will inherit a royal eternal kingdom in God's perfect paradise one day! Romans 8 assures you that you are a child of God led by the Holy Spirit. And your heavenly Father-King is not just some distant kind of dad. No, He's the kind you can run to for a big bear hug. He loves and cares for you and doesn't want you to live in fear about anything. You can have all courage and all confidence when you focus on the promises of God, trusting that you will share in the greatness of Jesus Christ and His kingdom forever.

> Dear God, You are my King and You are my heavenly Father. I'm so grateful to be Your child! Please keep me focused on Your promises, and make me bold and brave with Your power and love all the time. Amen.

You Might Need Help with Prayer

The Holy Spirit helps us in our weakness. For example, we don't know what God wants us to pray for. But the Holy Spirit prays for us with groanings that cannot be expressed in words. And the Father who knows all hearts knows what the Spirit is saying, for the Spirit pleads for us believers in harmony with God's own will.
ROMANS 8:26–27 NLT

Sometimes when you pray, you feel anything but gutsy. You might feel silly or weak or overwhelmed or clueless about what to say. That's totally okay! Let Romans 8 encourage you that God knows your heart and everything you think, say, and do. And the Holy Spirit inside you knows how to tell God all about what you're going through and what you need.

Dear God, sometimes it's hard to know what to say to You or how to ask for help. I'm grateful that Your Holy Spirit is praying for me in perfect ways that I never could. Thank You for knowing me so well and taking such good care of me! Amen.

Gutsy Is Good; Lazy Is Lame

In the name of the Lord Jesus, keep away from any Christian who is lazy and who does not do what we taught you. . . . We did not eat anyone's food without paying for it. We worked hard night and day so none of you would have to give us anything. . . . When we were with you, we told you that if a man does not work, he should not eat. We hear that some are not working. But they are spending their time trying to see what others are doing. Our words to such people are that they should be quiet and go to work.

2 THESSALONIANS 3:6, 8, 10–12 NLV

We absolutely need some time in life to rest and have fun and not think of the hard things that require gutsiness. But we have to be careful that we don't take *too* much time for that R & R. We don't want to become lazy. What does this scripture tell us about being lazy compared to being a hard worker?

> Dear God, please bless me with relaxing, restful times,
> but also help me never to become lazy. Show me the
> good work You want me to do in gutsy, strong ways.
> Help me to find joy in both work and relaxation. Amen.

Joseph Was Gutsy

[Joseph said,] "As for you, you meant evil against me, but God meant it for good, to bring it about that many people should be kept alive, as they are today. So do not fear; I will provide for you and your little ones." Thus he comforted them and spoke kindly to them.
GENESIS 50:20–21 ESV

Take some time to read Joseph's story in the Bible, and let it remind you that God can take the very worst situations and turn them into blessings. He can take anyone's evil plans toward you and turn them around for your good. It doesn't get much worse than being sold by your siblings into slavery in another country like Joseph was. And that was just the sad beginning! Yet God used the awful experiences Joseph endured to bless him. Whatever you are going through today, no matter how hard it is, choose to be loyal and obedient to God like Joseph was, and in His perfect timing God will reward you for your faithfulness.

**Dear God, remind me of Joseph's gutsiness and
loyalty and obedience to You, even in the midst
of cruelty and injustice. I believe You can take
anything that's meant to harm me and turn
it into good. I'm trusting You. Amen.**

Little Things, Big Miracles

*"There is a boy here who has five barley loaves and two fish, but what
are they for so many?" Jesus said, "Have the people sit down." Now there
was much grass in the place. So the men sat down, about five thousand
in number. Jesus then took the loaves, and when he had given thanks, he
distributed them to those who were seated. So also the fish, as much as they
wanted. And when they had eaten their fill, he told his disciples, "Gather
up the leftover fragments, that nothing may be lost." So they gathered them
up and filled twelve baskets with fragments from the five barley loaves left
by those who had eaten. When the people saw the sign that he had done,
they said, "This is indeed the Prophet who is to come into the world!"*

JOHN 6:9–14 ESV

Jesus performed an amazing miracle with just one little lunch from one
little boy. And the boy was kind and gutsy to give up his whole lunch for
Jesus to use. Remember this story anytime you might be wondering why
you matter and what God can do with you. He loves you, and His power is
working in you to do the good works He has planned.

**Dear Jesus, remind me every day that You can use even
the smallest things to create the biggest miracles! You are
amazing, and I'm so glad I know and love You. Amen.**

Fear God and Stand in Awe of Him

Let all the earth fear the L<small>ORD</small>; let all the
inhabitants of the world stand in awe of him!
P<small>SALM</small> 33:8 <small>ESV</small>

If you've ever been to a natural wonder like Niagara Falls or the Grand Canyon, you probably know what it's like to respect and be in awe of something that is so big and awesome that people never could have created it—something that just blows your mind. You respect the great danger posed by giant waterfalls and huge canyons if you should happen to fall into them, and you also think of how incredible they are and how amazing it is that they exist! We should fear God with awe and respect in the same way, knowing that He is capable of danger because He holds all power, but we should also be grateful that He loves us dearly as His children and will ultimately always protect us with forever life. Proverbs 19:23 (<small>NLT</small>) says, "Fear of the L<small>ORD</small> leads to life, bringing security and protection from harm."

Dear God, I stand in awe of You! I fear You in the best
sense of the word. I love and respect You with all my heart.
Please keep growing me in love and respect for You! Amen.

Think about Such Things

Whatever is true, whatever is noble, whatever is right,
whatever is pure, whatever is lovely, whatever is admirable—
if anything is excellent or praiseworthy—think about such things.
Whatever you have learned or received or heard from me, or seen
in me—put it into practice. And the God of peace will be with you.
PHILIPPIANS 4:8–9 NIV

What do you watch, read, and listen to on television, on the internet, in books and magazines, and through music and social media? It all matters. It all affects who you are and how you think and talk and act. The world will try to tell you that even the bad stuff is all just for fun, but don't listen to the world; listen to God, especially through His Word. In the book of Philippians, the apostle Paul said to keep our minds thinking about what is true, noble, right, pure, lovely, admirable, excellent, and praiseworthy. Whenever you put a thought or idea into your mind from what you watch, read, or listen to, ask yourself if it matches up with this scripture.

**Dear God, help me to obey Your Word and be careful about what
I allow into my mind through the many forms of entertainment
and media in the world. I want to be gutsy about staying
away from the bad and focusing on what is good. Amen.**

Have the Guts Not to Give Up

Do not let yourselves get tired of doing good. If we do not give up, we will get what is coming to us at the right time. Because of this, we should do good to everyone. For sure, we should do good to those who belong to Christ.

GALATIANS 6:9–10 NLV

Sometimes we feel *so tired* that we want to give up on following God and His Word. We watch people who don't care a thing about loving God and others yet seem to live pleasurable lives without consequences—and that can totally discourage us. It can tempt us to be like them or to get really depressed. So we have to remember that God's Word tells us not to get weary of doing good. If we don't give up on following Jesus, God will bless us at exactly the right time with exactly the things that He knows we need and will give us true joy forever.

Heavenly Father, I need Your help not to become weary and give up on doing good. Please encourage me and remind me that the main reason I do good things is to make You happy because You love me more than anyone, and I want to obey You as a way of showing my love back to You. Amen.

Focus on Real Beauty That Lasts

*Do not let your beauty come from the outside. It should not
be the way you comb your hair or the wearing of gold or the
wearing of fine clothes. Your beauty should come from the inside.
It should come from the heart. This is the kind that lasts.*

1 PETER 3:3–4 NLV

Through television and social media and magazines, the world and all its celebrities and influencers will try to tell you what beauty is. But you will only weaken your courage and confidence if you constantly try to keep up with them. So be gutsy and ignore them. Instead, focus on what God's Word has to say about real beauty. It comes from the inside, from the heart. You probably know people who look gorgeous on the outside but sure don't act beautifully. And you probably know people who don't follow any of the beauty and fashion trends yet are truly beautiful from the inside out because of all the goodness, kindness, and love that shine from them. Which type of person would you rather be—one who focuses on outward beauty or one who focuses on inward beauty? Only one kind of beauty will last. Only one kind of beauty matters to God.

**Dear God, help me to focus not on what I look like and
what I wear on the outside but on beauty that comes
from my heart because I love and follow You. Amen.**

The Greatest Gutsiness Ever, Part 1

[Jesus] prayed more fervently, and he was in such agony of spirit that his sweat fell to the ground like great drops of blood.
LUKE 22:44 NLT

There is no greater gutsiness than when Jesus willingly suffered and gave His life on the cross to save people from their sin. Jesus had cried out desperately to God in the garden of Gethsemane just before He was arrested and then crucified. He asked His Father if there might be another way so that He didn't have to suffer. But He also said to God, "Do what You want, and not what I want."

Jesus was willing to do anything the Father wanted because He knew God's ways are always best and always working for good for people who love Him. And in this case, God was working through Jesus' suffering to save people from their sins. The gutsiest act of all time was also the saddest act of all time—because Jesus was guilty of nothing, yet He took on all our sin. But it was also the most loving act of all time.

Dear Jesus, You willingly gave Your life to save all who believe in You from their sin. Help me to boldly share what You did to give us eternal life so that more and more people will know You as Savior. Amen.

The Greatest Gutsiness Ever, Part 2

As they stood there puzzled, two men suddenly appeared to them, clothed in dazzling robes. The women were terrified and bowed with their faces to the ground. Then the men asked, "Why are you looking among the dead for someone who is alive? He isn't here! He is risen from the dead!"

LUKE 24:4–6 NLT

The greatest gutsiness of all time ended with the greatest victory of all time—when Jesus conquered death forever by coming back to life. Only the one true God could accomplish such a miracle! And because we have the hope of victory over death, we can live fearlessly! God, the almighty Creator, is our loving heavenly Father. He sent His Son, Jesus, to teach us how to live our lives and to be the payment for our sins, and He gave us the Holy Spirit to be with us and guide us constantly until we live forever in heaven. We have everything we need because of Jesus' work on the cross, and because of His Holy Spirit in us we can live each of our days courageously.

Dear Jesus, there aren't enough words for how grateful I am for the greatest act of gutsiness the world has ever known! I praise You and I love You! Amen.

Hold On Tight

"A man who tells what is going to happen or a dreamer of dreams may come among you. . . . But if he says to you, 'Let us follow other gods (whom you have not known) and let us worship them,' do not listen. . . . For the Lord your God is putting you to the test to see if you love the Lord your God with all your heart and with all your soul. Follow the Lord your God and fear Him. Keep His Laws, and listen to His voice. Work for Him, and hold on to Him."
DEUTERONOMY 13:1–4 NLV

God knows you can handle tests in your life, gutsy girl. He will give and allow them to see if your faith in Him as the one true God is real and if you love Him with all your heart and soul. So follow God, obey Him, work for Him, and listen to Him. Hold on tight to the only one worthy of your complete devotion.

> Dear God, I want to do a great job showing You how much I love You and believe in You. I never want to stop holding on tightly to You! You alone offer real salvation from sin because You sent Your only Son to die for my sin and rise again to conquer death forever. You alone are worthy of all my faith and worship. Amen.

Watch for Little Glimpses

*"No eye has seen, no ear has heard, and no mind has imagined what God
has prepared for those who love him." But it was to us that God revealed
these things by his Spirit. For his Spirit searches out everything and shows
us God's deep secrets. No one can know a person's thoughts except
that person's own spirit, and no one can know God's thoughts except
God's own Spirit. And we have received God's Spirit (not the world's
spirit), so we can know the wonderful things God has freely given us.*

1 CORINTHIANS 2:9–12 NLT

What do you dream about the future? And what do you dream about heaven?
As you dream, remember 1 Corinthians 2:9–12. We can never fully imagine
how awesome the good things God has planned for us are! But if we stay
strong in our faith in God, we can ask the Holy Spirit within us to show us
good glimpses. What good glimpses are you seeing from God these days?

**Dear God, I trust You have amazing plans and blessings for my
future—both here on earth and forever in heaven. Show me
glimpses, please! I'm so excited for Your perfect plans. Amen.**

Gutsy Love Comes from God

God is love. God showed how much he loved us by sending his one and only Son into the world so that we might have eternal life through him. This is real love—not that we loved God, but that he loved us and sent his Son as a sacrifice to take away our sins. Dear friends, since God loved us that much, we surely ought to love each other.

1 JOHN 4:8–11 NLT

Knowing that someone loves you gives you courage and so much more, doesn't it? You know that whatever happens in life, good or bad, you have someone to give you a hug, to encourage you, to remind you of all the good things in life and all the ways you are blessed and cared for. If you have even just one person loving you, supporting you, comforting you, and cheering you on, you have much more courage, strength, and confidence. Don't ever forget that all those good things ultimately come from God. He is love itself, and He is the source of every good and perfect gift.

**Dear God, You are the source of all real love.
Thank You for showing us what love is and
letting people love one another. Amen.**

Throw Off Everything That Hinders

*Therefore, since we are surrounded by such a great cloud of witnesses,
let us throw off everything that hinders and the sin that so easily entangles.
And let us run with perseverance the race marked out for us, fixing our
eyes on Jesus, the pioneer and perfecter of faith. For the joy set before
him he endured the cross, scorning its shame, and sat down at the right
hand of the throne of God. Consider him who endured such opposition
from sinners, so that you will not grow weary and lose heart.*

Hebrews 12:1–3 NIV

Are there things in your life that keep you from doing what you should, like this scripture talks about? Do you spend too much time doing dumb stuff that doesn't matter instead of the good things that God has planned for you? It's a challenge for everyone, and we all need to have the guts to look honestly at our lives to see what keeps us away from God's will—and get rid of those things. Thankfully, the Holy Spirit is happy to help!

Dear God, please help me see what I need to throw out of my life—anything that keeps me from doing Your perfect will. Help me to run the race You've planned for me in the very best way I can! Amen.

Never Defeated

[Jesus said,] "The thief comes only to steal and kill and destroy;
I have come that they may have life, and have it to the full."
JOHN 10:10 NIV

We can feel relieved and confident because of the fact that no matter what the devil tries to do to us, we will always win against him in the end. He might hurt us or make us stumble away from God at times, but he will never totally defeat us when we trust in Jesus as our Savior. This scripture tells us that the devil wants to steal and destroy every good thing, but Jesus came to give us life to the fullest. When Jesus died and rose again, He showed that absolutely nothing the devil does can ever defeat the powerful love of God and His desire to give us everlasting life with Him!

> Heavenly Father, thank You that Jesus rose to life again after being crucified. He is proof of Your gift of eternal life for me. Nothing can ever take away that gift, and that makes me feel gutsy and brave! I will watch out for and stand against the devil, who will try to tear me away from a close relationship with You. I'm glad he can never actually defeat me because I am always safe and secure with my Savior. Amen.

Shipwrecked, Part 1

*[Paul said,] "Take courage! None of you will lose your lives,
even though the ship will go down. For last night an angel of the God
to whom I belong and whom I serve stood beside me, and he said,
'Don't be afraid, Paul. . . . God in his goodness has granted safety
to everyone sailing with you.' So take courage! For I believe God.
It will be just as he said. But we will be shipwrecked on an island."*
ACTS 27:22–26 NLT

Paul was on a ship in a horrible storm, and his words to the crew and other passengers were both comforting and scary. We might wonder, *Why did God let them shipwreck at all?* We don't know for sure all the reasons why. But we can use this story as a reminder that God never promised to keep us from every scary circumstance. Even in the midst of threatening situations, though, He can save our earthly lives. And what He does promise is heavenly life forever when we trust in Jesus as our one and only Savior.

**Dear God, I don't always understand what You're doing and
why we have to go through hard times. But I want to keep
trusting You anyway, and I know You ultimately save and
give forever life to everyone who trusts in Jesus. Amen.**

Shipwrecked, Part 2

Once we were safe on shore, we learned that we were on the island of Malta. The people of the island were very kind to us. It was cold and rainy, so they built a fire on the shore to welcome us.

ACTS 28:1–2 NLT

Paul and everyone on board the ship were safe, just as the angel of God had promised. And we see how God provided for their needs through the kind people of the island that they landed on. No matter what awful things we might have to experience in life, God will always provide good people to help us through them. Ask God to show you these blessings. Notice and thank the people who help you through hard times in both big and small ways. Praise God when you see Him working through others to take good care of you. And because you have seen God take care of you in the past, you can be gutsy when facing any future hard thing.

Dear God, thank You for always providing for my needs and bringing me helpers in every kind of situation. Amen.

The Powerful Act That Proves Our Faith

This letter is from Paul. I am a servant owned by Jesus Christ and a missionary chosen by God to preach His Good News. The Good News was promised long ago by God's early preachers in His Holy Writings. It tells of His Son, our Lord Jesus Christ, Who was born as a person in the flesh through the family of King David. The Holy Spirit proved by a powerful act that Jesus our Lord is the Son of God because He was raised from the dead.

ROMANS 1:1–4 NLV

You can be gutsy about sharing your Christian faith because no other religion promises what Jesus promises, with the proof He gave of rising from the dead. Paul started out the book of Romans by stating clearly that Jesus is the Son of God and that people everywhere should put their trust in Him. The Holy Spirit "proved by a powerful act"—raising Jesus from the dead—that Jesus truly is the Son of God. This is why we know today that following Jesus Christ is the one true way to know God and have eternal life.

Dear God, thank You for the powerful act of raising Jesus from the dead. You are the one true God, and You alone are worthy of my faith. Help me to share Your truth! Amen.

He Takes Away Fears

I will honor the Lord at all times. His praise will always be in my mouth. My soul will be proud to tell about the Lord. Let those who suffer hear it and be filled with joy. Give great honor to the Lord with me. Let us praise His name together. I looked for the Lord, and He answered me. And He took away all my fears.

PSALM 34:1–4 NLV

If you've ever been in a bad car accident, you might struggle with a fear of driving. If you've ever been bitten by a dog, you might have a fear of dogs. If you've ever had a close call with tornadoes or hurricanes, you might be scared of more bad weather in the future. For sure, our scary experiences in the past create some of the fears we have now. But God knows each of us individually very well. He knows all about every hard, sad, and scary thing we've ever endured. He knows every detail about us, down to the very number of hairs on our heads (Luke 12:7). So we can admit our fears and let Him take them from us and fill us with His peace instead.

Heavenly Father, You know exactly the reasons I struggle with certain kinds of worries and fears. Please comfort and encourage me in the specific ways I need so that I can overcome my anxiety. Amen.

Even When You're Weak, Afraid, and Shaking

When I came to you, I did not preach the secrets of God with big sounding words or make it sound as if I were so wise. I made up my mind that while I was with you I would speak of nothing except Jesus Christ and of His death on the cross. When I was with you, I was weak. I was afraid and I shook. What I had to say when I preached was not in big sounding words of man's wisdom. But it was given in the power of the Holy Spirit. In this way, you do not have faith in Christ because of the wisdom of men. You have faith in Christ because of the power of God.

1 CORINTHIANS 2:1–5 NLV

Paul admitted that he was weak, afraid, and shaking sometimes when he shared with others about Jesus. Can you relate? Then let Paul's example encourage you. He was scared sometimes, and he didn't feel like he had all the best-sounding words and wisdom that would make everyone want to listen to him either. Paul just knew about Jesus. Paul knew Jesus had transformed his life, and Paul knew that Jesus died on the cross and rose again to save people from their sin and give them eternal life. It is the power of God working in you through His Holy Spirit that helps you share the good news of Jesus. To be truly gutsy, all you have to do is let God work through you!

Dear God, it's all You! Please work through me to help others know You and trust Jesus as Savior. Amen.

Get Deeper and Stronger

It is good to hear that your faith is so strong in Christ. As you have put your trust in Christ Jesus the Lord to save you from the punishment of sin, now let Him lead you in every step. Have your roots planted deep in Christ. Grow in Him. Get your strength from Him. Let Him make you strong in the faith as you have been taught. Your life should be full of thanks to Him.
COLOSSIANS 2:5–7 NLV

Let God lead you step-by-step in life through the power of the Holy Spirit. No matter how strong your faith in Jesus is right now, it can always get stronger. No matter how deep your roots are into Christ, they can always go deeper. The deeper the roots of a tree go, the stronger it is. The deeper its roots grow, the harder it is for the tree to fall. The same goes for you. The deeper your roots grow in Jesus, the stronger you are in your faith and the harder it is for any difficulty or pain in life to make you fall.

Dear Jesus, please keep me growing deeper roots in You with stronger faith each day as You guide my every step. Amen.

Seek Real Joy, Not Just Happiness

You make known to me the path of life; you will fill me with joy in your presence, with eternal pleasures at your right hand.
PSALM 16:11 NIV

Our feelings change quickly. Something that made you happy last year or even a month ago might seem silly or boring now. So real joy is always much better than temporary happiness. Let these scriptures help teach you about real joy:

- "I have placed the Lord always in front of me. Because He is at my right hand, I will not be moved. And so my heart is glad. My soul is full of joy" (Psalm 16:8–9 NLV).

- "Though you have not seen him, you love him; and even though you do not see him now, you believe in him and are filled with an inexpressible and glorious joy, for you are receiving the end result of your faith, the salvation of your souls" (1 Peter 1:8–9 NIV).

- "The joy of the Lord is your strength" (Nehemiah 8:10 NLV).

Dear God, help me to remember that feelings and happiness change easily, but joy that is true and constant is always found in You! Amen.

Soar High on Wings Like Eagles

Have you never heard? Have you never understood? The LORD is the everlasting God, the Creator of all the earth. He never grows weak or weary. No one can measure the depths of his understanding. He gives power to the weak and strength to the powerless. Even youths will become weak and tired, and young men will fall in exhaustion. But those who trust in the LORD will find new strength. They will soar high on wings like eagles. They will run and not grow weary. They will walk and not faint.
ISAIAH 40:28–31 NLT

When you feel exhausted and nowhere near gutsy enough for any good work, remember that God has endless strength and energy. If schoolwork, tough friendships, a stressful family life, health problems, or anything else at all is draining you, take time to focus on this scripture. Wait patiently for God to come to your rescue and make you rise up with wings like an eagle! What a magnificent thought!

Dear God, I am so, so tired. And I'm so glad that You never are. Please give me Your energy, strength, and courage to keep on going and to overcome. Help me soar high on wings like an eagle! Amen.

Don't Turn Away from God

"I will tell how they are to be punished for all their sin. For they have turned away from Me and have given gifts to other gods, and worshiped the works of their own hands. Now get ready. Stand up and tell them everything that I tell you. Do not be afraid of them."
JEREMIAH 1:16–17 NLV

After King Josiah died, the nation of Judah turned almost completely away from God. So God called the prophet Jeremiah to warn the people of Judah about the punishment, trouble, and suffering coming their way. At first Jeremiah was too anxious and afraid to obey God, but then God gave him a powerful pep talk (read it in Jeremiah 1:6–10). Jeremiah's warnings remind us today never to turn away from the one true God and His perfect ways. We will face bad consequences if we do. God wants us to worship and serve Him alone, and He always knows and wants what is best for us.

Dear God, help me to remember the warnings from Jeremiah. Please help me never to turn away from worshipping and obeying You. Amen.

Why Do You Look to the Sky?

After [Jesus] said this, he was taken up before their very eyes, and a
cloud hid him from their sight. They were looking intently up into the sky
as he was going, when suddenly two men dressed in white stood beside
them. "Men of Galilee," they said, "why do you stand here looking into
the sky? This same Jesus, who has been taken from you into heaven,
will come back in the same way you have seen him go into heaven."
ACTS 1:9–11 NIV

After Jesus died on the cross and then rose to life again, He returned to
earth for forty days to prove Himself alive and to teach His followers more
before going up to heaven in a cloud. His friends kept watching the sky, but
then two angels appeared and wanted to know what they were doing. Yes,
Jesus promised to return someday, but it was time for His followers to get
busy sharing about Jesus. Do you ever wish Jesus would hurry back now
too? All Christians can relate. But while we wait, we also need to keep busy
sharing the good news that Jesus died to save us from our sin and that He
is alive now and will take all who trust in Him to heaven someday.

Dear Jesus, I'm watching the sky for You, eager for
You to return, but I also want to keep busy sharing
Your good news until You do come back. Amen.

Jesus Loves to Save

Two robbers were crucified with [Jesus], one on the right and one on the left. And those who passed by derided him, wagging their heads and saying, "You who would destroy the temple and rebuild it in three days, save yourself! If you are the Son of God, come down from the cross."... And the robbers who were crucified with him also reviled him in the same way.
MATTHEW 27:38–40, 44 ESV

Both of the thieves who were crucified with Jesus mocked and ridiculed Him, according to the book of Matthew. But in the book of Luke (23:39–43), we read that one of the thieves must have changed his mind. He admitted his own sins and knew that Jesus had done nothing wrong. He chose to believe in Jesus and asked Jesus to take him to heaven. And Jesus promised that the man would be in paradise with Him that very day. Jesus wants all people to repent of sin and believe in Him, and He gives every chance for salvation up until a person's very last second of life here on earth.

Dear Jesus, help me to be gutsy and brave to tell others about You by sharing how much You love to save anyone at any moment. Help me to help others see their need to admit their sin and put their trust in You as our only Savior. Amen.

Wait for the Lord, Be Given the Earth

Do not want to be like those who do wrong. . . . Trust in the Lord, and do good. . . . Be happy in the Lord. And He will give you the desires of your heart. Give your way over to the Lord. . . . Rest in the Lord and be willing to wait for Him. Do not trouble yourself when all goes well with the one who carries out his sinful plans. . . . For those who do wrong will be cut off. But those who wait for the Lord will be given the earth.

PSALM 37:1, 3–5, 7, 9 NLV

We might read this scripture and get really frustrated because sometimes it seems like the ones who do wrong *are* the most successful. But it's not true, even if it looks that way on the outside or according to what's popular in the world. Do your best to ignore those who do wrong. Stay far away from their sin and their plans. Follow God's plans and wait for Him to bless you instead.

Dear God, help me not to want to be like those who do wrong. Help me to focus on loving and obeying You. I trust You to bless me, not according to what the world says is success but according to what You say is success. Amen.

The Lord Is Your Shepherd, So Fear No Evil

The LORD is my shepherd, I lack nothing. He makes me lie down in green pastures, he leads me beside quiet waters, he refreshes my soul. He guides me along the right paths for his name's sake. Even though I walk through the darkest valley, I will fear no evil, for you are with me; your rod and your staff, they comfort me. You prepare a table before me in the presence of my enemies. You anoint my head with oil; my cup overflows. Surely your goodness and love will follow me all the days of my life, and I will dwell in the house of the LORD forever.

PSALM 23 NIV

Psalm 23 provides strength, courage, and peace in good times and bad. No wonder it's one of the most famous passages of the Bible! It boosts our hope and eases our anxiety to read and remember the truth that God leads us and cares for us like a good shepherd here on earth—until the day we're with Him forever in heaven.

Dear Lord, thank You for the many ways You lead, love, and care for me. Thank You for being my faithful good shepherd through all of life's paths, both rocky and smooth. Amen.

It's Going to Be More Than Okay

We know that in all things God works for the good of those who love him, who have been called according to his purpose.
ROMANS 8:28 NIV

"It's going to be okay." Have you ever heard those words and hated them? Sometimes it can feel like the person saying them to you during a rough time doesn't truly know or care about your problem and/or pain and how awful life feels in the midst of it. That's when remembering Romans 8:28 is so necessary. If you love God, are trusting in Jesus as your Savior, and are living for Him, God is working in every kind of situation—even the hardest and weirdest and most painful ones—and truly will make everything okay in the end. And not just okay, but so much better than we can ever imagine, when we are eternally with God on the new earth someday.

It's understandable that we all sometimes feel like nothing will ever be okay again in this sinful and crazy world, and so we need to be reminded of the truth of God's Word every day!

Dear God, when I'm in pain and confusion and feel discouraged and everything opposite of gutsy and brave, remind me that You are always working for the good of those who love You. I love You, and I trust You. Please keep holding tight to me. Amen.

Jesus Is Alive!

The angel said to the women, "Do not be afraid, for I know that you
are looking for Jesus, who was crucified. He is not here; he has risen,
just as he said. . . . Then go quickly and tell his disciples: 'He has
risen from the dead and is going ahead of you into Galilee. . . .'"
So the women hurried away from the tomb, afraid yet filled with joy,
and ran to tell his disciples. Suddenly Jesus met them. "Greetings,"
he said. They came to him, clasped his feet and worshiped him.
MATTHEW 28:5–9 NIV

Sometimes when we're feeling down or anxious and need an extra dose of
gutsiness, we need to focus on three simple words: Jesus is alive! That is
the basis of our faith. Jesus rose from the dead, and if that were not true,
then our faith would be useless (1 Corinthians 15:12–19). Can you imagine
being one of the women who were dear friends of Jesus who first saw Him
after they'd watched Him die on the cross? It had to be the most astonishing
surprise to hear the angel's news and then meet up with Jesus, who was
not dead anymore but alive again! That powerful news is what we still trust
today. Jesus is not dead. He is alive!

Dear Jesus, I know You are alive, and You give me
all the hope and courage I need for this life. Amen.

Let Nothing Move You

*[God] gives us the victory through our Lord Jesus Christ.
Therefore, my dear brothers and sisters, stand firm. Let nothing
move you. Always give yourselves fully to the work of the Lord,
because you know that your labor in the Lord is not in vain.*
1 CORINTHIANS 15:57–58 NIV

As you keep maturing, of course you'll change your mind on some things here and there. Tastes and preferences and activities change with time. Look at fashion styles now and in the past for just one example! Minor things are fine to change your mind about, but there's one thing to be gutsy and stubborn about forever—trusting in Jesus Christ alone to save you from your sin, give you eternal life, and bring you to heaven one day.

Dear God, I never want to change my mind about this: I believe You alone are the one true God, and Your Son, Jesus, is the only way to eternal life in heaven because He died on the cross and rose again to save me from my sin. And I believe I have the power of the Holy Spirit in me to do the good works You created me to do here on earth until one day I'm forever in Your presence. Help me to truly follow Your Word and live confidently in Your truth and share it with others. Amen.

Scripture Index